THE TENDER GIFT
Breastfeeding

THE
TENDER GIFT
Breastfeeding

DANA RAPHAEL

SCHOCKEN BOOKS • NEW YORK

First published by SCHOCKEN BOOKS 1976
Second Printing, 1976

Copyright © 1973 by Dana Raphael

Library of Congress Cataloging in Publication Data

Raphael, Dana, 1926–
   The tender gift.

   Bibliography: p.
   Includes index.
   1. Breast feeding. I. Title.   [DNLM: 1. Breast feeding—Popular
works. WS120 R217t 1973a]
[RJ216.R33 1976] 649'.3   75–24267

Foreword by MARGARET MEAD

Dr. Dana Raphael has devoted a decade to painstaking study of the problems of breastfeeding and mothering the mother, which she discusses in this book. She has examined the literature on primitive cultures; she has done research in our own culture and in Europe; she has observed the behavior of other creatures. But where in the past anthropological research was directed mainly at insight-giving, she has gone a step further in a new use of anthropology—culture-building. She has asked the question, How can we adapt our contemporary style of life to provide the support which a new mother, especially the new mother of a first baby, needs in order to care for, nourish and cherish her baby? Basing her suggestions on painstaking research and then experiments, which she has made herself, she advances the conception of doula (pronounced doola), the nurturing other woman, which most societies provide for new mothers but which the current United States culture often fails to do.

The women's movement today embraces two groups, those who wish to permit women to be more fully maternal and fully feminine, and those who wish to use modern biological and medical technologies to eradicate as many vestiges of our evolutionary past as possible. The first group, to which Dana Raphael and I emphatically belong, would like to remove many of the constraints on enjoyable and effective motherhood which modern obstetrical practices have introduced. She recognizes that not all mothers will want to breastfeed their babies, and that in some cases this is not possible, but she believes that it is important to provide support for all those who do.

This is a practical book as well as a sound one because the author has done extensive and responsible research; it is practical because she does not advise anything, including breastfeeding an adopted baby, which she has not tried herself.

Margaret Mead
The American Museum of Natural History

5

INTRODUCTION

There are so many books on breastfeeding available today that one might wonder if indeed everything has not already been said about this womanly art. So it should be pointed out that "The Tender Gift—Breastfeeding" is not so much a book of techniques as it is a rather comprehensive survey of breastfeeding, past and present, in many cultures and even among animal groups.

But that is not all, for in doing her research, Dana Raphael also discovered why so many mothers of today, herself included, are not always able to nurse as successfully as they would like to. She found that regardless of how simple breastfeeding looks . . . "all you have to do is put the baby to the breast!" . . . it can be much more complex in actual practice, and especially so for mothers living in a culture where the majority of babies are bottle fed. So important is this concept that she devotes several chapters to explaining the need for and ways to go about "mothering the mother" while at the same time providing the encouragement and support that is as important as a knowledge of nursing techniques. It is these chapters, I feel, that make the book especially valuable reading for all people genuinely concerned with helping the breastfeeding mother, whether this is on a professional level or simply as relatives and friends.

Marian Tompson
President, La Leche
League International, Inc.

ACKNOWLEDGMENTS

My deepest respect and gratitude go to Margaret Mead, who gave me what I call my "scholarly feet." She was the source of encouragement and intellectual excitement which propelled me into ever new searchings. Her energy, provocative insights and generosity have been major motivations for this study and a great model for many other aspects of my life.

My admiration goes to Morton Fried, whose brilliant teaching added to my love and understanding of anthropology. And I owe much to Conrad Arensberg, also my professor at Columbia University, whose intellect has been a constant stimulus and delight. His conceptualization of patterns and universals pervades this entire work. To him also goes credit for perceiving my ideas of mother-becoming as "matrescence."

Thanks to Gladys Walker for her excellent editing of this work; to Bea Fogarty, for her willingness to research the whole library if need be; and to Angela Holland for her help in matters of style and for her sweet way of never saying "no."

Other important contributions were made by Doctors Albert Schwartz, William Kueffner, and Frank Scholan and, at University College Hospital in London, by Mavis Gunther, Sheila Ranson, Elizabeth Tylden, Norman Morris and the many midwives —such artists in their work.

The Sister-midwives at L'Hotel Dieu de Gaspé (Canada) also gave of their time and energy, as did Pierre Vellay, M.D., in Paris. Betty Ann Countryman and Marian Tompson from La Leche League International read the manuscript and made many interesting suggestions.

I offer appreciation to the many mothers—Mary Rassias, Lee Greaney, Vidal Clay, those in the Connecticut La Leche League branch (especially Jane Freund), and all who adopted and breastfed infants and responded so cooperatively to my questions;

—to the dozens and dozens who gave me hours of honest and sensitive responses to my interviews in the United States, Canada, London, Paris and India;

—to Magdalena Tomajek who helped me mother mine;

—to Tom Head, a severe critic, and Sally Bates, a patient one;

—to Eleni Rassias for the word "doula";

—to my sons: Brett, who started me on this research, and Seth, who showed me why I should spend so many years working at it;

—to daughter Jessa who gave reasons for it all with her vitality, beauty and spirit.

Finally, I deeply thank my journalist husband, Howard, a great editor, who was there with creative support and genuine encouragement at those times when this mother needed mothering.

CONTENTS

A Personal Note to the Reader

Like magic it happened. With a surge, three days after the birth of my first child, my breasts became distended with milk. I had naively assumed throughout my pregnancy that when the infant arrived I would automatically be ready to feed him, and that it was as simple as that. But my joy turned to anguish as the baby screamed angrily when there was not enough milk. Little did I know that I had begun the terrifying cycle so familiar to many mothers who had tried for the first time to breastfeed.

When the baby was but a week old, I became *really* anxious. The baby cried louder. I strained to feed. The baby got nothing, and I got more frightened. Finally, screaming with frustration, the baby turned away. Panic-stricken, I did the one thing I had promised myself I would never do. I prepared a bottle.

The "magic" of breastfeeding? As far as I was concerned it was more like sorcery, for without warning, a short time later my milk disappeared altogether. In desperation, I asked myself what went wrong. Despite, or rather because of my sorrow and disappointment at my failure, I was determined to study everything I could find on breastfeeding—to find that elusive magic. I vowed that with my next child it would be a different story. And it was.

I went first to the medical literature, to doctors, and then to nursing mothers for some understanding. When they all failed to supply the answers, I turned to my chosen discipline, anthropology, and began what was to be fifteen years of intensive research on breastfeeding in animals, in our own culture and in more than two hundred other cultures. I found my answers. In fact, I did my research so thoroughly that ten years after my last natural child, I nursed an adopted baby.

The results of my work, with particular attention to the subtle and largely forgotten art of "mothering the mother," I now pass along to those women who want the very special relationship

with their babies that only breastfeeding permits. In this book, I
explain those factors which determine success and warn of the
path that leads to failure. I offer the new mother the information
she needs to create a supportive environment so that she can
enjoy this most rewarding aspect of motherhood.

DANA RAPHAEL
Director
The Human Lactation Center, Ltd.

1

When Mothers Need Mothering

Mothering—Who Needs It?

WHEN A BOTTLE-NOSED DOLPHIN GIVES BIRTH TO A CALF, OTHER adult females in the group help out by keeping her offspring afloat until he can fend for himself or until the mother regains her strength. In a rather similar way, adult female elephants, who live in closely related family units of females with their young, are supportive of each other especially during labor and delivery, creating an ideal setting into which each calf is born. These acts of caretaking increase the survival chances of that herd (Iain Douglas-Hamilton, personal communication, 1972). Animals seem to know the value of mothering.

In the case of human mothers, those who have some sort of "mothering" from another person do well at breastfeeding, but those who do *not* can almost certainly expect trouble.

In most cultures of the world, girls get married, get pregnant, deliver and breastfeed as a natural part of their participation in society. Built into their world is a very special kind of support they need to fulfill this role. These women are aware that breastfeeding is not automatic. They know how fine the thread is between their milk and their babies' lives. They know how delicate the balance is between breasts that will and breasts that will not "let down" their milk.

Today, most American mothers begin nursing without any idea that they might have a hard time. They think that breast-feeding is simply going back to the natural and the pure, and that it can be the same as it was in grandmother's day. But they are wrong. In the past, a new mother often stayed in her bedroom. The baby was tucked in with her, and the mother was coddled and firmly directed by loving women who had nursed their own infants and knew all about it.

All this has changed. When grandmother walked out of the nursery to take up painting, politics and bridge, the whole cultural tradition of pampering *mother* along with baby went out with her.

Few people in a modern mother's circle know what breast milk looks like. No one is there to tell the new mother how to hold the nursing infant, how long to keep him sucking, or how to care for uncomfortably full breasts or irritated nipples.

In most countries, women usually decide what is right or wrong for infants. In America, we prefer to leave the responsibility to medical authorities, who are usually male and often uninformed about some simple, even critical aspects of breastfeeding. Their answers are sometimes medical prescriptions for problems that are social and emotional. For instance, one doctor suggested that the mother consult an ear-nose-throat specialist for a baby described over the phone as choking at the breast. One quick glance at the nursing pair by someone who *knew* would have revealed that she was holding the baby in a smothering position. But these days, who ever sees a woman breast-feeding?

At home and but a few days out of the hospital, the new mother comes to the awful realization that she and her hungry infant are going to have to make it alone. In such an isolated and nonsupportive environment, the breastfeeding mother is almost certainly condemned to an anxiety—milk-loss—failure syndrome.

Luckily, there is an unlimited supply of cow's milk available, so the baby lives. The woman, already full of doubts about her adequacy as a mother and her competence in breastfeeding, is quite easily convinced that bottles are her only alternative.

On the other hand, many women feel relieved not having to breastfeed, and it is a grave error to make them feel guilty because they do not. They are better mothers if they can remain at a slight distance and have less intense physical contact with their babies. They too must be permitted their choice.

But the woman who wants the intensity that breastfeeding offers can have it. Breastfeeding can be accomplished if she appreciates the climate of the time, is wary of the attraction of the bottle, understands the process of lactation, remembers the benefits to her baby and herself, discounts the folklore which predicts trouble, and, above all, makes sure she herself gets some mothering.

2

Becoming a Mother

Motherhood—A Rite of Passage

A FRENCHMAN, ARNOLD VAN GENNEP (1909), COINED A PHRASE, *rites de passage*, to describe the ceremonies and rituals—marriage, birth, death, circumcision, graduation, ordination, etc.— that mark special changes in people's lives. These are the occasions and celebrations that highlight life's great transitions.

A woman's most critical *rite de passage* occurs when she becomes a mother. The tremendous change that happens when a female passes, as a result of pregnancy and childbirth, from woman and wife into the state of motherhood, is a major life crisis and should not be taken for granted. Childbirth brings about a series of very dramatic changes in the new mother's physical being, in her emotional life, in her status within the group, even in her own female identity. I distinguish this period of transition from others by terming it *matrescence*° to emphasize the mother and to focus on *her* new life style.

This very special change of role is often obscured by putting all the emphasis on pregnancy and birth (really only a *part* of matrescence) and then by spotlighting the baby. Becoming a

° Professor Conrad Arensberg capped my concept with this excellent term.

mother, with a whole shift of activity and a new way of life, is often underemphasized. On the contrary, a woman in this *matrescent* state should be highlighted and this particular period singled out as unique and important. The infant should not be allowed to upstage his mother at this critical time, especially because his whole future depends on how she accepts her new role.

The Tikopia of the Solomon Islands recognize this difference (Firth 1956). They herald the birth of a child by announcing "a *mother* has given birth." We say "a *baby* is born."

My research (1966) into the records of over 250 cultures for information on this matrescent period uncovered a great variety of behavior in the rules, rites, and restrictions that accompany this change-over. Some of them are enormously complex, involving long chants or lists of rules. What was found to be important was not what the songs say or the customs forbid, but *who* is doing the singing or forbidding. It isn't a question of whether gods, ancestors, trees, or devils are called up for help but rather whether someone is there to do the calling. The effect that person's presence has on the mother makes all the difference.

For instance, we want to know if it is the husband's duty to burn incense and chant songs during his wife's delivery. We care less about what he sings. Our main concern is how important his presence is to his wife's well-being.

It does not matter whether it is the father's mother, or the mother's mother who is expected to bring the mother food and drink, or which of the mother's co-wives is expected to stay and help, or if it is her sister who usually does this job. What concerns us is that one of them is *supposed* to be there, and that by prescribing who that person should be, the people in that particular culture are *taking care of their mothers*.

Some groups make more of a fuss over their mothers than others do but all show some concern. It may very well be that a closer look will show that the greater the concern for the mothers, the better the survival chances of the infants.

Let's analyze the whole stage of matrescence. Let's see when it begins, how long it lasts, who is involved, and how the involvement of others with the mother works to keep her infant alive.

When Does a Mother Become a Mother?

A surprising find was that the birth of the baby does not necessarily pinpoint the moment of motherhood. Something called "social maternity"—a time determined by social practice—is often a more important determining factor.

Many people ignore nature's physiological signals. They make their own rules. This happens, for instance, with the interpretation of "maturity." In Rome a child is considered an adolescent while she is physically very much a child. Parisians, on the other hand, delay calling their girls young women longer than most people, and well past the time when the physical changes of puberty occur (Van Gennep, 1909).

Maternity is also subject to cultural interpretation. In America a swirl of controversy revolves around the unborn child. The question is, at what point does he become human? Though each infant is considered "complete" at birth, he is thought to be human even before this. The time most generally accepted is when the embryo becomes a fetus at three months. The moral outcry of murder often follows abortions that occur after this period. Obviously, what is conceived as a bundle of cells or considered a human being is a matter of social decision.

In America a female is a mother in theory but not in practice as soon as she delivers an infant who survives, even if it is premature. However, there is an exception where maternity is denied despite physiological birth. That occurs when a woman, married or unwed, gives up her infant for adoption. Since motherhood implies taking care of a child and since she has never done this, she can think of herself as never having been a mother.

In some societies, a wife must give birth to an infant of the preferred sex before she is granted motherhood status. For instance, in a culture where girls carry on the family line, a woman giving birth to one boy after another doesn't do honor to herself or her group. On the other hand, ask a woman from the Middle East how many children she has, and she will tell you how many *sons* she has. Daughters, though loved, don't make a woman a mother.

Sometimes a woman doesn't become a mother until the baby is considered "human"—another one of those cultural decisions.

This usually coincides with an age when the infant's chances for survival seem assured. In some groups, life is so hard that the infant is not granted full humanity for months, even years. In a way this practice is a kind of emotional defense against the trauma that accompanies the extremely high infant mortality rate still found over much of the world. If the infant is thought of as something not yet human, his death may then be accepted with less torment by his kin group.

In many cultures the process of becoming a mother and the baby's maturing often go on simultaneously. As the infant loses his "newborn" qualities, the fuss around the mother subsides, other adults withdraw little by little, and the mother slowly assumes her new status.

For the American woman, full matrescence is supposedly acquired the moment she leaves the hospital—abruptly, with little training and less support—three to five days after delivery. Sad to say, this happens sooner here than anywhere else in the world and long before most mothers are ready for it.

Cushioning the Mother

Many other cultures ease the mother into her new role in significant ways. First her activity is curtailed. She may be forbidden to work, cook, lift, stand up, sing, even feed herself. In some cultures, she may be so immobilized that she is expected only to take care of her elimination needs. This makes it mandatory for her to have other people around to do her chores.

Although the new mother and the experienced women around her may not be aware of it, much of what goes on in practice and ritual includes a lot of practical teaching on how to care for her infant.

All of these interaction patterns—whether educational, religious, or merely supportive—seem to help the mother to gear herself practically and emotionally for her new role *(and, at the same time give her a chance to establish her milk supply and sensitize her to her infant's needs)*.

Who's Supposed to Help?

Rules always exist as to just who may interact with the mother and who may not. In Western cultures, children are usually separated from a new mother because supposedly the less they know and the less noise they make, the better. Yet, in the Philippines it is not unusual to have children around even during the delivery. In some cultures the father's presence is *required* during ceremonies or even during the actual birth, but it is more usual to leave matters in the hands of other women, especially older ones.

Unfortunately, in the United States, because there is no one else to do them, chores such as cleaning, laundry, shopping, etc., are often relegated to an already overworked husband after his working day. This puts pressure on both parents at a time when they are already under the strain of learning their new roles. Frequently the result is a resentful new father and a guilt-ridden mother.

This is not the first time in American history that fathers were forced into the picture. In frontier America the situation was even more critical. A hard-pressed husband, with no women around to assist his wife at childbirth and afterward, would often find himself burying his wife as well as his infant.

The role of men in the birth and the postpartum period varies around the world. Over half of the 250 cultures in my study do not allow men at the birth scene. Some peoples feel it is improper, others that it is downright dangerous for them to be there. Some even prohibit the husband from seeing the mother or child anywhere from a few days to many months after delivery. However, since the birth of a child usually elevates a man's position in society, this may compensate him a little and help him bear some of the lengthy prohibitions.

Around the world, mothers prefer to have their mothers or sisters play the "mother's caretaker" role. This is not surprising. These are the most likely candidates for tenderly easing the mother into her new status. To a lesser extent, the husband's mother is supposed to help out, but more often it is her duty to care for the new infant while others care for the mother.

The Keystone . . . The Doula

The most common pattern is for females to care for other females, whether they be dolphins, elephants or human beings. (Possibly, women in general are more comfortable in these roles than men are, but it does not mean that all women are good at them but may be better doing other things, playing other roles. But there is no question that some men make superior caretakers of children.)

We have adopted a word to describe the person who performs this function—the *doula*. The word comes from the Greek, and in Aristotle's time meant "slave." Later it came to describe a woman who goes into the home and assists a newly delivered mother by cooking for her, helping with the other children, holding the baby, and so forth. She might be a neighbor, a relative, or a friend, and she performs her task voluntarily and on a temporary basis.

It is in the latter context that we use the term "doula" as a title for those individuals who surround, interact with, and aid the mother at any time within the perinatal period, which includes pregnancy, birth, and lactation.

The function of the doula varies in different cultures from a little help here and there to complete succoring, including bathing, cooking, carrying, and feeding. Whatever the doula does, however, is less important than the fact that she *is there*. Her very presence gives the mother a better chance of remaining calm and nursing her baby. In areas such as the United States, where new mothers are often isolated from their kin, the doula's help is crucial if the mother wants to breastfeed. Her care and handling could save the day. Her presence could save the mother's milk.

We might add that the doula, though most frequently female, experienced and often older, can also be a man. Though inexperienced and young, he may possess the critical ingredients that make the difference—a willingness and ability to be supportive.

Recuperation—the Long and Short of It

Just how long does a new mother need a doula's help? Again, it is usually not the physical well-being of the mother but the cultural rules of society which determine the length of time.

Frequently this recuperation period coincides with time units used in other activities. For instance, forty days is the period of special religious observations in Moslem rituals. Forty days is also considered the proper duration for the new Moslem mother to remain isolated, pampered, and exempt from work.

In the United States, we take two-week vacations, give two-week advance notices, etc. It is not surprising, then, that we think it sufficient if a new mother is inactive for only two weeks. Actually, postpartum "recuperative" periods reported around the world vary from a minimum of one week to as much as two years. In almost all the societies analyzed, some care was always given to the new mother, and in most of them her activities were limited and her needs ministered to for at least several weeks.

What is the best method to determine when a mother becomes a mother? Watching the behavior of others toward her, especially those who play the role of doula, can give the best clues. By noticing the kind of aid the doula gives the mother we get an idea of the current status of her needs and her matrescence. When we no longer see the doula, we can be fairly sure that the woman's initiation into motherhood is complete.

Matrescence is a time of coddling. It is a period in life when most of the disturbances and pressures on the new mother should be avoided. This is the doula's most essential job. Insulation gives the mother the peace of mind and the relaxation of body she needs to care for and breastfeed her infant.

That's what most mothers around the world can expect. That's the ideal set-up. Let's see now how near the American mother comes to this picture when it is her time to bear young.

3

The American Way of Birth

IN SOME CULTURES, PEOPLE ASSUME THAT A BABY WILL BE BORN when it is good and ready, so they make sure that someone is with the mother-to-be for a long period before delivery (Mead 1965). Without benefit of medical advice, they know how important it is to be supportive of the mother.

The net effect, of course, is that the woman feels safe, cared for, and "mothered" even before the baby arrives. She is literally surrounded and nurtured during her labor, delivery, and the postpartum period. Sometimes, as with some American Indian groups, husbands are essential to a successful delivery especially when they are expected to perform the *couvade*° which focuses evil on them and away from their wives. In the case of the Manus of New Guinea, it is considered critical for an experienced and very strong-willed women to preside and make sure all goes well.

The person who is to be informed at the first sign of labor is well-known in most cultures. Everyone is aware of the signs of imminent delivery (contractions every few minutes, etc.). Most

___

° A further description of the *couvade* will be found in Chapter 10.

women know well in advance where the baby will be delivered, who will act as midwife, who will supervise the rituals and check on the mother's physical needs, and who will care for her needs once she has had the baby. In societies where there are close kinship patterns, people live with or near each other, and it is not difficult to bring all the principals in this drama together quickly.

Not so in the United States. Americans care for their mothers very intensely at one level but are totally indifferent at another. The mother's physical care during hospital delivery is excellent, but the emotional care given her during pregnancy, in childbirth, and at home later leaves much to be desired.

Going It Alone

This uncomfortable climate is partially a result of our most common family pattern—the nuclear family made up solely of parents and their offspring. Not only are these units usually isolated economically and emotionally from most of their kin; they are also often widely separated geographically. Young couples frequently find themselves in new jobs that take them to faraway locations, where no one is a relative and all their relationships are new.

Without friend or kin, these young people start off with nothing but worries. The mother-to-be herself must work out the way she will get to the hospital, a worry which is worsened by her fear that her baby may not arrive "on time." A husband's vacation, a doctor's dinner party, or the complete redecorating of the baby's room may determine whether the infant is a "good" baby and comes into this world on schedule, or whether he is "bad" and comes early.

People expect the pregnant woman to behave as if she were "well." It is usually up to her to plan everything and to consider all the alternatives. Will a car be available? Can her husband be near home at that time? Is there a generous neighbor who might respond to her call in an emergency? Does a subway or a bus run by the hospital all night? Will her doctor get there on time so that she will see at least one familiar face? Her anxiety about these uncertainties may become greater as her date approaches and she begins to realize how alone she is, how much she must do on her own. Is it any wonder that the American expectant mother often feels abandoned both emotionally and physically?

This kind of conflict results in part from the premium American women place on independence. In Puritanical fashion, reinforced by the sporadic and dramatic women's liberation movements of this century, she is expected to pride herself on the fact that she needs *no* help, that she can get to the hospital alone, that she can remain alone during most of her labor, that she can grin and bear down during contractions, and that subsequently she can hang onto this precious independence by managing alone when she gets home.

Nonsense! This whole concept is totally unrealistic. Furthermore it is inhuman and often the cause of breastfeeding failure, postpartum blues and breakdowns, and other extreme anxieties that should not be a part of this unique period of intense intimacy and warmth.

The Hospital Stay—A Half-hearted Attempt

Despite twenty years of positive experience with "rooming-in," most hospitals still separate the baby from the mother. Hospital routines allow the mother to see and feed her infant only on schedule. Many mothers feel that this separation is painful.

Usually only the nurses and the mother are permitted to handle the baby. The exceptional hospital allows the father close contact with his wife and newborn during and after birth. Generally his presence is regulated by limited visiting hours. The new baby's grandparents are equally scheduled, if indeed they are included at all.

If the new mother has decided to breastfeed and asks for help from the hospital staff, the information she receives may be brief, academic, and all too often just plain inadequate. Unlike cultures where the only persons permitted to be with the mother are the most recently delivered females in the group, American mothers look to nurses who may be medically well-trained but are often young, unmarried, and inexperienced in the emotional side of delivery and the practical aspects of breastfeeding.

Many nurses have no preference—the bottle is as good as the breast, they believe. Certainly bottle feeding by the nursery staff is easier for them in that it takes the problem off their hands. However, decisions should not be made on the basis of convenience but rather on the needs of the nursing pair. And again, just as obstetricians, not mothers, deliver babies, and pediatricians, not grandmothers see to their care, so nurses, not mothers are responsible for their feeding. It is realistically impossible for the nurses to maintain intimate contact with each infant in the nursery—to hold, feel and have time to sense each individual baby's rhythm and needs. So, feeding measurable ounces on schedule, is expedient and solves the problem.

Not all nurses are pro-bottle or anti-breastfeeding. But even when the nursing staff *is* honestly affirmative toward the breastfeeder and comfortable with the breastfeeding method, the nature of the hospital routine may undermine success. Time and again, supplementary hospital feedings of water and/or milk given to quiet the infant have been proved to be associated with lactation failure. The infant is often spoiled for breastfeeding. Mother's nipple—smaller, more pliable and harder to milk—is less desirable than the bottle's super teat, from which the milk flows so easily. After just a few chances at the bottle, the infant often rejects the breast.

Instant Motherhood

The new mother doesn't have a chance in the hospital to achieve matrescence. Strangers are in charge not only of her baby but of her as well. For a few days she is completely dependent upon them. Then suddenly they disappear. In an instant, as she rises from the wheel chair, as she goes through the hospital doors and the nurse hands her the infant, the American woman becomes a Mother. No matter how unsure, inexperienced, or fearful, this neophyte, only a few moments ago in a dependent patient role, is handed a live bundle and sent off to mother it.

Where Experience Counts

It is significant that among some nonhuman primates the *experienced* females get to hold the infants of others the longest. In most human societies, too, experienced women closely supervise young mothers who may be but a few years from childhood themselves. This arrangement provides a stable framework that helps the new mother adjust to her new role.

In our culture, to the contrary, the new young mother is often left without an experienced companion, mature adult, or even a friend.

Lacking knowledge of customs and child-raising practices, she tends to bungle her way through as best she can. But her best is often not good enough.

Infants quickly sense the difference in handling between an experienced and an unsure person. One obvious example of insecure mothering is the colicky baby, who frequently has an equally "colicky" mother. Pediatricians have noted that these are often first babies with nervous new mothers. The indecisive handling by a tense mother may lead to digestive problems, which in turn create more tension in the mother, louder screaming by the infant, further anguish in the mother, a more severe case of colic, and often an injured relationship. It should not surprise us that many women break down.

Postpartum Depression

In their study of postpartum depression (1960) Doctor Richard Gordon and his nurse wife, Katherine, ran two special forty-minute instruction periods for a group of women attending antenatal classes. They were concerned with the social and psychological adjustments women must make when entering the matrescent stage. Another group, with whom these women were to be compared, were not given these short but important sessions.

Only 15 percent of the women who had the extra help in understanding their new role had postpartum emotional upsets. But 37 percent of those women who didn't have this special briefing did have postdelivery crises.

More important, the new mother who had no previous experience with babies, had the least help available to her, and had recently moved to a new neighborhood, was the most prone to postpartum distress. When her social environment was deliberately rearranged so that she got help from a *dependable* person (a doula), her mental state showed dramatic improvement. The Gordons could actually correlate their patients' successes or failures with geography. They found that the *incidence of postpartum breakdown increased with the actual distance in miles of the new mother from her own mother, sister, or close friends.*

It is a vicious cycle, upsetting enough for the bottle-feeding mother, but dangerous for the breastfeeding woman, for it creates a climate that will lead to milk failure. All this could be avoided with the introduction of an experienced woman—a doula—into the picture, whose responsibility it would be to shield the mother.

The next chapter shows how this works.

4

The Secret Weapon

Why Some Fail

EVEN WHEN A MOTHER IS NURSING WELL IN THE HOSPITAL, continued breastfeeding is not assured. Once home, she must assume the partnership implicit in the American nuclear family arrangement and take charge as mother, wife and housekeeper. In addition, even if she has chosen to breastfeed, she is almost certain to be exposed to many coercive situations. Often she is not only doomed to fail at breastfeeding but, lacking direction and instruction, she is likely to find it hard to adjust to her new motherhood role.

Many people think that breastfeeding success is simply tied to the attitudes a woman has about herself as a female. This is by no means the whole story. In a study I made of English and American mothers (1966), all the women interviewed who were attempting to breastfeed were generally happy about their maternity. All of them were comfortable with the idea of breastfeeding and sincerely motivated to do it. Few had any inkling that there might be difficulties. With their positive attitudes, theoretically these mothers should have had no problems. But many did.

Excerpts from the interviews tell the sad story:

33

"I was having trouble nursing and my mother-in-law came to stay. She told me how she had expressed her extra milk into a cup just for fun and the next morning it was three-quarters cream. Cream! My milk looked so watery. I gave the baby her first bottle that day. When she drank three ounces, it was the beginning of the end."

      °   °   °   °

"My sister-in-law gave birth two weeks after I did. Her baby was on a bottle and my mother kept comparing our two. This made me very nervous. I was terrified that I was starving my baby, but I was afraid to mention it because I didn't want to stop nursing. I never told anyone else, but one night I dreamed of a funeral and it was my baby's. I had starved it to death. The next day I started with supplementary bottles. In two weeks I had no more milk."

      °   °   °   °

"I stayed with my mother for the first baby. We didn't get along. I only breastfed for three weeks."

      °   °   °   °

"A friend helped me after I came home from the hospital. Neither she nor my sister approved my nursing. But I did fight it for one month."

      °   °   °   °

"I had a lovely nurse for five whole weeks. After she left it seemed everything fell apart. Everyone was against my continuing. A few days later Curtis was on bottles."

Surprisingly, mothers with a strong desire and a great excitement about breastfeeding were just as prone to fail as were those with less passion for the whole idea. My survey also revealed that a number of other common concerns—the amount of love a mother felt for the infant, her level of concern about his health, her susceptibility to breast abscesses or engorgements—all had very little or nothing to do with success or failure. What did matter was the amount and type of help new mothers received after they left the hospital. Mothers without help or with help that was insufficient, hostile or coercive were quick to lose their milk. Their lot was a long-lasting sense of failure.

The Winning Side

I found that the trend toward failure could be reversed when a doula arrived, or that success was nearly assured if one was there in the first place. Mothering by the doula greatly determined the level of the mother's milk supply.

Excerpts from interviews identify the presence of a doula and convey the pleasure of a positive experience.

"With my first baby I was frightened when the milk came in, and I didn't nurse at all. When the second baby came, my mother stayed with me a few days until the nurse came. Mother didn't like the whole idea of breastfeeding, but the nurse did, and she helped me for three weeks. I nursed Richard for months after."

o   o   o   o

"My mother was very helpful. She stayed with me for two weeks. My in-laws and my husband were so proud that I was breastfeeding. I fed June for six months without any trouble."

o   o   o   o

"With my first child my mother helped me. She knew everything, and I breastfed for eight-and-a-half months."

o   o   o   o

"I was distraught and about to give up. I most certainly couldn't have gone on if my father (a physician) hadn't stepped in and encouraged me."

o   o   o   o

"Neither my mother nor my mother-in-law was any help. The nurse I had was jealous that I took over the most important part of the baby's care. My husband was interning at the time and felt

very involved with the baby and me. He saw to it that everyone behaved. Even though my pediatrician was negative, Bill said to go on. I nursed our baby for seven months."

In all of these successful experiences the presence of others after childbirth and the quality of interaction between the mother and her doula during this period were the deciding factors.

The Rare Male Doula

Not surprisingly, few of these effective doulas were male. Husbands and doctors, in general, came least recommended, even though there were some excellent male supportive figures.

One reason why a husband's potential as a doula is limited is his absence from home for the major part of the day when help is most needed. A two-week vacation is the maximum most young men can hope for, and this is not usually enough time for the mother to get organized and establish a synchronous relationship with her infant.

Besides this, the husband may be struggling as he adjusts to some of the responsibilities and changes implicit in his new role as a father. New fatherhood (I call it *patrescence*) is not always as simple as passing out cigars. The pressures he must handle might not make him a negative influence, but they could restrict his effectiveness as a doula.

How Much Do Doctors Help?

None of the women in this study were able to use their obstetricians or pediatricians as their supporting figures—their doulas. This doesn't mean that supportive physicians do not exist, nor that they couldn't do the job of playing doula at a distance. But often pediatricians think of breastfeeding as part of becoming a mother and therefore in the obstetrician's province, whereas obstetricians believe it is related to the baby's hunger and of pediatric concern. If a troubled mother calls the obstetrician she can be given hormones to dry up her supply, while if she telephones the pediatrician, she may come away with formulas and the latest in bottle gadgetry. What is needed is some old-fashioned knowledge on how to improve the milk supply.

But let's not put undue blame on the physicians, for they too are caught up in a culture which is biased toward bottle feeding. Besides, even a doctor who favors breastfeeding (and many of them do) has a limit to his available time. Often it is this very lack of time which forces him to turn to the expedient bottle. After all, almost the total responsibility for the infant's life has been transferred from the mother and other adult women to him. That's quite a heavy burden to carry. In any one week a pediatrician may have to deal with as many as fifty newborn infants and their concerned mothers.

Just one call each from a few nursing mothers is too much to add to an already heavy daily telephone load from the parents of sick children. As a result, the bottle (which never dries up) is an appealing and almost essential prescription. The preferable mother/patient becomes the one who feeds that measurable amount of quality-controlled milk through a sterilized bottle to a thriving baby whose weight gain shows up well on a chart.

This critical situation will only straighten out when healthy baby care and sick baby care are separated—when the well infants (and children) are cared for by specially trained non-professionals thus relieving physicians to care for the ill.

As it now stands, since breastfeeding is not an illness, it gets shortchanged in the medical curriculum. One pediatrician admitted, "Only one two-hour lecture on breastfeeding was scheduled during my training." Guiltily he added, "I was absent that day!" But even had he been present, his knowledge of breastfeeding would not be anywhere near complete. In fact, the ejection reflex, the critical determinant of whether or not the baby gets milk, still remains a mystery to many.

There is also an attitude about breastfeeding being "natural," which is used to explain away why some women can and some cannot do it. By clinging to this "natural" mystique, many doctors don't have the impetus to keep up with medical procedures which deal with lactation.

For example, pediatric journals stressed some years ago that nipple pain and damage are much more prevalent among women who scrub their nipples or use alcohol as an antiseptic before nursing than among those who don't (Newton 1952). Many doctors still recommend such sterilization, treating human nipples as they would a rubber teat.

Another problem is the engorged breast. When such a condition occurs, many doctors immediately stop the mother from nursing. A better way to treat milk engorgement has been well researched (Newton & Newton 1952). The baby is encouraged to nurse *more* frequently in order to relieve the tension in the breast. Even cases of severe engorgement have been treated successfully this way and without interrupting lactation. The Newtons (1950b, 1962) also suggest another method of treatment which is to have the mother feed from one breast, while milk ejection is caused in the engorged breast by injecting the mother with the hormone oxytocin (Pitocin).

The resources are there, but physicians still rely on the concept that if this method of feeding gives any trouble at all, the solution is to prescribe the bottle.

An end to breastfeeding may be an easy alternative for a doctor to recommend to a mother who fears she is starving her baby or whose breasts are painfully sore. But the physician is seldom aware of the emotions or the trauma of failure that go with such advice. For the breastfeeding woman, the psychological ramifications run deep. Many women burst into tears at the recollection of their deep disappointment when advised to abandon breastfeeding. They often harbor these sorrowful emotions for years.

Such an emotional crisis is not necessary. Virtually all women can have a successful breastfeeding experience. The general American idea is that a woman lactates successfully only if she is able to breastfeed a healthy, weight-gaining baby for at least six weeks without difficulty. Any mother who is made to feel that a specific number of weeks or months of breastfeeding is required for success has one more strain put upon her. The length of time she breastfeeds should be a conscious and deliberate act of *her* discretion. When it is made into an incredible numbers game, it often becomes a nightmare.

When Is It Success?

Success for an American mother cannot be judged alone by the fact that her baby survives, which is the obvious criterion for success in primitive and underdeveloped countries. With or without breastfeeding, most American babies live. Mothers can stop nursing whenever they like. A mother in India or Africa, however, cannot wean much before two years. Only then would she be willing to believe that her infant will live. Measuring breastfeeding in years, not months, is as natural to these mothers as it is a wonderment to Western women.

An American mother who has breastfed for only three weeks (or six weeks or three months) and has stopped because she wanted to can be considered successful. The only criterion, where fortified food and sterilized milk are easily accessible, is her contentment, excitement and joy. We will notice a similar pattern later on when we discuss the nursing of an adopted child. Here the quality of nourishing rather than the quantity of nourishment is what counts.

Some day something called "biological success" may be pinpointed to an exact day or month. This would be the optimum time of most benefit to both mother and child. For now, however, in cultures where bottles are not available or safe, success demands several years of breastfeeding, while in bottle-safe Western societies success is when the mother says so.

Women who lactate successfully in most societies of the world are generally unconcerned about how long they will continue, how many minutes they feed on each breast, whether or not to supplement, and when to do so. When the baby is hungry he is fed. As long as the mother and her infant fit both emotionally and physically, there is usually plenty of milk, the baby lives and the milk supply adjusts itself to the child's growth and intake.

Behind this idyllic picture are the reasons why it works. In most cultures definite regulations for new mothers run for a time period spanning weeks, months, and sometimes as much as a year after childbirth. The mother's daily bath, her every mouthful, her seclusion in one room or in a special hut, her choice of companions, even her interaction with her husband are all strictly regulated.

This separation and seclusion are rationalized as necessary because the mother is "unclean" for a period after delivery, because she might endanger her milk supply by breathing the outdoor air, or because her particular magical state might be dangerous to others.

No matter how unscientific the rationalizations, they are believed and followed and they serve the purpose, which is to set this period aside as a special time. The whole focus is on and around the mother, which results in making her a relaxed and successful breastfeeder. The fuss, the fêtes, and particularly the doula all make this possible.

In most areas of the world breastfeeding and motherhood are inseparable and joyfully accepted. The doula's job is less to fight outside influences than to take care of the mother's personal and immediate needs. In the United States the physical care of the new mother is taken care of by physicians, flush toilets, automatic washers and other accoutrements of a technological society. One function of the doula is to stand between her and the bottle-dominant, often hostile culture she must be sheltered from and to provide a warm atmosphere within which she can breastfeed and joyfully experience her matrescence.

5

The Great Myths

AMERICANS DON'T TAKE KINDLY TO THE SUBJECT OF BREAST-
feeding. I discovered this while trying to understand the attitudes surrounding the breastfeeding mother. I wanted to know
exactly what she was up against and what she had to deal with
in our bottle-feeding society. So I went out and asked questions.

It's too early to ask anyone *anything* at 7:02 A.M., and my initial question, put to unsuspecting rail commuters, opened many
a tired eye.

I would slide quietly into a seat beside a conservatively
dressed man just beginning to peruse his morning paper as the
train sped him toward the city and begin, "May I ask you a question? What do you think about breastfeeding?"

I went about and selected people from as many ethnic and
economic groups as I could find. Everyone was fair game. I
pulled out my notebook as I rode with cabbies, lunched with fac-
tory workers, questioned shoppers, or chatted with loungers on
park benches.

I asked my opening question hundreds of times to men and
women alike. I was often eyed suspiciously. People usually

couldn't believe they had heard me correctly, asked me to re-
peat myself, and then still didn't seem to believe the question.

When the answers finally did come, they reflected doubt, uncertainty, and a great deal of misinformation. Many truly needed
time to think because it was such a new and an uncommon subject to them.

Baby, Mom and the Great Debate

I found that when people approve of breastfeeding, they use
the baby's health and comfort as a prime reason. Mother's milk
makes a baby healthier, stronger, and more content, they tell
you. Or it gives him immunities to various diseases.

Those who argue against breastfeeding usually take the mother's side, citing the many discomforts that she must endure. She's
confined, inconvenienced, depleted, they say. Some charge that
she is more prone to infection, abscesses, even cancer.

Whether for or against breastfeeding, most people qualify, ra-
tionalize and justify their points of view with opinions they really
believe to be "fact." My survey clearly shows that professional
and lay people alike harbor and nurture emotionally charged
misconceptions about breastfeeding, and that most discussions
on the subject are overwhelmingly dominated by fiction, hear-
say, and colorful but questionable folklore.

This is true of those who praise it as well as those who con-
demn it. The most important thing is one's opinion and arguing
it out. The infant's welfare seems secondary to winning one's
point. Breastfeeding is for debating, not doing.

The Male Reaction

Men are less decisive and more inclined to claim to have no
opinion at all, at least at first. I often recorded such comments as,
"It's up to the wife." "I'm a man, how would I know? I never
tried it." "The doctor decides, anyway."

Some men, frankly embarrassed by questions about breastfeeding, countered with, "That reminds me of a dirty joke." And
they had to tell it to me.

Breastfeeding to many men is not associated with babies or
feeding at all. Breastfeeding means breast, and breast means sex.

Many repeatedly proved this by emphasizing the erotic. It was frequently easier for them to describe intimacies about their sex lives than to continue a discussion about feeding a baby.

Many, reflecting extreme discomfort in talking about the subject, showed great hostility. One man retorted, "Breastfeeding? I'd cut off my wife's tits if she ever tried it!"

These reactions are extremely significant. They clearly indicate just how far we really are from accepting breastfeeding as a natural way of life or even connecting the breast with infant feeding at all. Breasts are for Daddy, not for baby.

A few social science students who promised to help me make this survey backed out at the last moment, further reflecting the confusion and embarrassment which often arises when this subject is raised. They explained apologetically that while they didn't mind questioning anyone about sex, they wouldn't be comfortable asking people about breastfeeding.

Sex apparently is a subject men enjoy talking about. Informants took the questions and their answers seriously. Queries about breastfeeding, confusing as it is with sex, are different, even unpleasant. Added to this is a lack of information that brings on embarrassment and defensiveness. Until these conflicts are sorted out, the climate will remain strained and confused.

The Female View

Women were equally as amazed by the initial question as were men, but they didn't respond with sexual innuendoes. Their answers were usually positive with conviction or negative with a vengeance. As discussions progressed, some became warmly moved, some openly hostile, some mildly guilt-ridden. But in any case, once stimulated, their interest was intense.

For instance, when I brought up the subject of the appearance of milk in the mother's breasts shortly after a baby is born, most women, including those who *did* breastfeed, admitted that they had never given any thought to this "miracle" of postpartum milk. It seems we take this sudden event for granted and believe that the breasts just "fill up" sometime after birth. We're not quite sure how soon or why three or four days after birth and not earlier. Since the American practice is for non-breastfeeders to be injected with milk suppressant drugs right after delivery it is not surprising that they really *don't* know when the milk appears.

Since breast milk is no longer the only way an infant can survive, women no longer have reason to discuss it or to question its source. A woman in America can give birth to her fourth child and honestly say, "Breastfeeding? I never thought about it."

Whenever I described the uniqueness of this complex physical process, most people reacted with amazement. It was indeed marvelous. "Does the milk I drink turn into my milk?" "Do small breasts produce less milk than large ones?" "How come my milk spurts out when the baby cries?" We often got into such an exciting discussion that it was difficult to end an interview. It was now *their* turn to question and my pleasure to teach.

The Association Game

Feelings about breastfeeding are revealed in different ways. Many people say they approve of it and they do, in the same sense that they approve of babies in general. A more direct question often got down to basic feelings and prejudices. I asked people what *animals* they associated with breastfeeding. (You, the reader, might want to close your eyes and answer this question before going on to read about what others thought about it.)

Answers to this query revealed more about a person's feelings and prejudices than any of their other comments. This was true particularly of those who were otherwise noncommittal.

The most common free associations were with cats, dogs and cows. Because these domestic animals are so familiar, such answers meant nothing in themselves. The clue was in the inflection. The answer "cow" could be said in a disgusted tone or in a pleasant voice, as when good old Bessie was associated with warm and fresh milk. Those who responded with lists of animals, and especially those who used diminutives like kitty-cat, puppy and piglet, showed strong approval.

All the exotic animals like wolf, tiger, ape, bear, were suggested by men and reflected not only originality, but aggressiveness.

The Breast Machine

I found that Americans typically equate the breast with a machine. They don't think of breastfeeding as a complex physiological process involving the whole body, but rather as "a method" which, like the bottle, can be turned on or off at one's convenience.

Discussions showed that a nursing woman is frequently judged by her ability to "produce." Like a good dairy cow, she too must be fed regularly. She must rest for a prescribed amount of time, be pressed into nursing on a set hourly schedule—an exact number of minutes on one breast and a greater but precise number of minutes on the other.

Those in the survey who talked about breast milk at all discussed it in production terms. There is either too little or too much of what is either too thick or too thin. Some worry about quality control, sometimes hand-expressing the milk into a glass and examining it, wondering if something should be done to change it.

The American Way

Even though some people prefer nursing, almost everyone was in accord that bottle feeding, not breastfeeding, is the "American way." I found that breastfeeding is even considered an "un-American" activity, something old-fashioned, foreign, often unwholesome. Both men and women used the same phrases when expressing extreme disapproval, "It's disgusting!" "Not for people!" "Animalistic!" "Not done!" Though it seems contradictory, even those who favor nursing often feel that bottle feeding is more sanitary and modern.

By the time most American children reach the middle grades, they are very much aware of how most of the systems of the body work. Not so with lactation. Nor are their teachers or parents much more knowledgeable. As a matter of fact, the degree of unawareness is sometimes astonishing.

One thirteen-year-old boy was shocked to realize during a discussion in a science class that he possessed two nipples just as women do. This realization led him to ask, "How does the milk in a woman's breasts come out?" He had seen paintings, many of them religious, of nursing infants, but he had never connected the breast with nipples, milk, or babies. Mouth–nipple contact had simply never occurred to him.

In most other cultures around the world, young boys grow up fully aware of breasts and their vital maternal function. They learn early that they will someday have to provide food so that their wives' breasts will fill with milk for their infants. Their sisters, who grow up holding real babies in their arms and nursing their dolls, know of no other way for babies to get food.

The American scene is quite different. American girls grow up believing that babies are fed from bottles and spoons. Women want to have a limited number of children, in quick succession, and get this sloppy babyhood stage over as painlessly as possible, so that they can get on with the business of doing something "important" with their lives.

A predominantly bottle-feeding environment must be seen for what it is—a threat to the woman who wants to nurse her infant. In order not to be swamped by this threat she must understand that the trend to bottle feeding is a human invention, not biologically controlled, and *in her case she can do without it.*

The next chapter explores how the trend to artificial feeding in a few decades became a way of life for a whole nation.

6

From Breast to Bottle
in Sixty Years

The Great Turnoff

CONSIDER THAT FOR MILLIONS OF YEARS MAMMALS HAD BEEN breastfeeding. Then, in just a fraction of a moment in time, the human animal changed this. We just turned off the breast!

Never in the evolution of any species has a bodily function been pressured into such a sudden and dramatic change. It could almost be compared to a mass rejection of sexual activity by the substitution of artificial insemination. Or the sudden introduction of intravenous feeding, which would make the mouth obsolete, at least for eating.

The physical change to artificial feeding actually requires only one generation. The social prerequisites, however, take much longer. Emancipation and comfortable economic conditions frequently go together and, in the case of the switch from breast to bottle, they certainly do. A reasonably settled existence and a constant source of food are minimum requirements before artificial feeding can become a way of life.

Time-Out for Mother

The great changeover, this take-over by the cow, began in America at the turn of the twentieth century and took but a few decades. Its roots, however, reach back more than a hundred years into the industrial revolution. Mechanization and mass production of goods gave a large number of women conveniences such as machine-woven fabrics, ready-made clothes, processed and prepared foods, and finally that greatest of all luxuries—time. Women found they could not only step out of the kitchen but out of the house as well. Why did they want to go out? What was so interesting out there?

First there was the exodus of women out of the home, very often to work. And, for the middle class who had servants, there was also entertainment in the form of movies, vaudeville, theater, dancing, and the company of other women. In addition there were all those mysterious things out there that men did—like politicking and making money.

Until the early twentieth century many women had little hope and less chance of ever reaching the world outside. Now they were magnetically drawn to it. Soon the idea took hold that no matter what was outside the home, it had to be more exciting than the day-to-day routine of child-raising and housekeeping.

This is not to say, of course, that these women sublimated their femininity, dropped their brooms, and deserted husband, home, and children. Nor does it mean that those who did strike off for new adventures did not love their offspring. It just means that some wanted more stimulation, and mass production of bottles helped to make it obtainable.

Up to that time breastfeeding was a baby's only means of getting food. The remaining child-raising duties could be relegated to others. Now, with the availability of the bottle, the mother's previously indispensable tie with her infant was severed.

The bottle suddenly took on a special aura which went far beyond its function. It stood for modernity, and "modern" in America meant "good." It symbolized liberation. Even when infants began dying of contaminated milk, it was inconceivable for mothers to believe that this new medically approved convenience could be at fault.

Enter the Cow—Milk and Trouble

For centuries, other forms of infant feeding had been used. Wet nursing and the feeding of animal milk are recorded in the world's Bibles. But these practices had always been an exception rather than the rule. Though royalty and upper-class women sometimes paid wet nurses in order to free themselves for other things, the general population resorted to group nursing, to passing the baby around if the mother couldn't nurse, if she was out working in the fields or if she died.

As more and more people adopted bottle feeding, the problems began to multiply. The rural dweller usually had a source of supply nearby. One cow for one baby was more than adequate, unless the cow was not milking, or she dried-up suddenly, or the calf and the baby had different birthdays.

If one lived in the city, there were more problems. The milk had to be transported long distances, and daily delivery was absolutely vital. In the summer, milk attracted insects and bacteria. In the winter it froze, and transportation broke down.

On top of this, if country dwellers were having trouble with quantity, city residents were having serious problems with quality. As cities grew and the country was pushed farther away, the transportation problem was solved by housing cows in the cellars of huge city buildings. Here there was no sunlight, no method of checking the milk or testing the animals.

As one can imagine, sanitary conditions were deplorable. Added to all this were the germs carried by the milkers, who were hired off the street—usually the poor, alcoholic, unwashed outcasts of the city. Looking back, there's little doubt why urban infants succumbed in large numbers.

The high infant death rate at that time was not entirely due to cow's milk. The industrial complex, with its crowding and disease, and the disruption and emotional isolation that comes when the large family breaks into small and widely separated groups, certainly contributed. Still, contaminated milk was a major killer.

Later on, vaccines and other factors unrelated to feeding helped to lower the death rate, but improved sanitary conditions and refrigeration were the prime contributors.

Even after a reliable delivery system for reasonably sterile milk was worked out, artificial feeding presented still another problem—getting the milk from milk can to baby's mouth.

Various types of containers were tried, including animal skins and glass blown bottles. But none of them were satisfactory. Milk, unlike wine and beer, doesn't have an alcoholic preservative to keep it from spoiling. It soured if left in the skin pouches. As for the bottles, they were often blown with narrow necks and eccentric shapes that were hard to clean. Any residue, even tiny amounts, quickly developed bacteria. If it didn't poison the baby, it gave him diarrhea, sometimes so severe that he was left weak and susceptible to other diseases.

Electric and gas refrigerators were not mass-produced in the United States as they are today nor adopted on a country-wide scale until after World War II, but women continued to switch to artificial feeding even though spoiled milk remained a constant hazard, often a lethal potion.

The Disappearing Grandmother

The grandmothering figure of the nineteenth century was gradually replaced by women whose own mothers were second generation bottle feeders. In just a few decades these women had become very proficient at sterilizing bottles, but if their daughters wanted to breastfeed, they no longer knew what to tell them to make it work.

The new grandmother's pattern was to help her daughter achieve independence and at the same time reserve freedom for herself. Everybody was pleased with this new way of life, little realizing that it spelled the end of the automatic, built-in grandmother. Suddenly there was no one to spoil and mother the mother, to baby-sit, discipline, love, cook, comfort, diaper or reassure by just being there.

Something had to fill the void for the new mother, and that something turned out to be a doctor/book combination. It had become normal for American women to turn to books for advice. Popular cookbooks of the nineteenth century contained miscellaneous sections with directions on how to swathe burns, clean off spots and wean babies.

This was a culture of young adults, often immigrants who, away from their own parents, had to learn many skills from other sources. Books were one resource. Coupled with this trend was a growing respect for the medical profession and a tendency to use physicians as authority figures for advice on matters way beyond medicine. Thus the combination of the right doctor and mass literacy spelled the beginning of bringing up the baby literally by the book.

Doctor Knows Best

A study of child-care literature of this century, with special attention to feeding habits, reveals some fascinating behavior patterns and reflects the massive changeover from breast to bottle.

Over the years the pendulum swings from a rigid to a permissive scheduling of infant feeding back to the rigid, then to somewhere in between, where it now hovers. Some of these swings are influenced by fads of the day, some by world conditions. War, peace, world competition, political crises, riots, scientific breakthroughs—all are interconnected with how people view their lives and think it best to rear their children. These trends can be followed by examining changes in even limited areas of behavior such as feeding schedules.

Since the editions of government publications on infant and child care are rewritten every few years, they are particularly useful in demonstrating and reflecting changing trends. The same goes for the writings of the eminent authorities who come into prominence during this period. Their writings and ideas change with the times as do the answers they give to those pressing questions mothers formerly resolved by asking the nearest older female.

The famous L. Emmett Holt, M.D., put out his first child care book in 1884. Later he was joined by his son, and for sixty years the Holt way was the "right" way. They were succeeded by Dr. Benjamin Spock, who came into his own in the forties.

It has often been asserted that one author or one book with enormous circulation could change the baby care and feeding habits of a nation. But this is not the way it works. The writings of a period reflect trends as much as they dictate them.

A good example of this is Spock, who is often blamed for having single-handedly invented "permissiveness." A closer look at the different editions of his famous *Common Sense Book of Baby and Child Care* (1945, 1957) shows that as times changed and the atmosphere fluctuated, so did he. His book became known as "the mother's bible" because he could understand and *respond* to the whims and needs of the millions.

Even strict Dr. Holt, who was all for breastfeeding and angrily against the bottle, gradually had to yield. Year by year his sections on the preparation and use of feeding formulas were enlarged.

The contents of these child-care books are exhaustive, and the tone ranges from dogmatic to intimate. The Holts (1927) *demand,* Spock *strongly suggests,* and the position of government lies between the two.

Government publications (U.S. Children's Bureau) of 1921 asked mothers to put their trust in nurses and doctors. "Doctor knows best" became the byword of the day. Two decades later, Dr. Spock hinted that mother just might know more than she thinks she does and should begin to trust her own judgment.

The Redoubtable Schedule

Spock's conclusion is not surprising when we follow the erratic changes in feeding schedule preferences over the years.

In a society where routines are so important in most areas of living—work, school, and even play—it's no surprise that eventually an infant's life, and especially his eating habits, had to be neatly compartmentalized also.

As early as 1894, Dr. Holt declared that infants should be fed every two or two-and-one-half hours. Wake the infant if need be, but keep the schedule.

Crying, too, was accepted as a necessary part of growing up. Holt didn't think crying hurt the infant. In fact, weeping fifteen to thirty minutes a day was said to be good for the child's character. This led naturally to the practice which surfaced in the twenties (with Watson, the behaviorist), of prescribing so many minutes of infant-holding per day and so many hours of adult/infant play per week. This philosophy persists to this day, whereby psychologists propose scheduling an infant's total life as he moves within air-controlled, glass-encased cribs.

As more and more babies were delivered in hospitals, it became necessary to put infants on a four-hour schedule which conformed to the nursing staff's eight-hour day. Conveniently, this worked out to two feedings per day per nurse.

It was easy for mothers to be convinced that such a program was best, for didn't the hospital authorities do it that way? So what started out as a convenience to the nursing staff ended up as a way of life for the infant.

It wasn't until years later that psychologists and physiologists began to talk about four-hour feedings as *unbiological*. Research showed that a newborn infant empties his stomach in one-and-one-half hours, not four, and that his hunger contractions are even more vigorous and painful than those experienced by a hungry adult.

It wasn't until later that an estimate was made on how much milk an infant might require. This was done by measuring the stomach capacity of several children, using the approximated average as the indisputable proper volume for every infant in the country. Differences in children and size were ignored. The hourly schedule was determined by the infant's weight. In the fifties, infants weighing seven pounds or more at birth were put on the three-ounce feeding every four hours regimen. Those who weighed less got to eat every three hours. Today, only infants weighing five and a half pounds or under get fed every three hours. The others, ready-or-not, get a fresh bottle every four hours.

Artificial timetables are imposed equally on the bottle and the breastfeeding mother, yet nothing could be more physically inappropriate to the latter. Nursing mothers need more frequent stimulation in the beginning to start the milk flowing and the breasts emptying. And babies on human milk, which is more efficiently and more rapidly assimilated, often require less milk but more frequent feedings.

But even though this information has been available for twenty-five years, to this day most hospital staffs and some nursing mothers stick to a four-hour schedule, fine for most babies, inappropriate for many. The endurance of the newborn is amazing!

Not everything about scheduling is bad. Some limitation, especially for the bottle feeder, is essential. The breastfeeding mother and her baby have a built-in self-regulating and self-limiting system. The baby nurses when he is hungry and the mother's milk supply quickly fits in with his need. The hungrier the baby, the more he will nurse, and the more milk will be produced.

Not so with bottle feeding. There is an unlimited supply of cow's milk and this could be too much of a good thing. Many infants will continue to suck out milk from a bottle even when they are bulging. Many mothers, imbued with the idea that the infant should determine when he has had enough, keep refilling the bottles. Overfeeding can lead to serious illness. Anthropologist Margaret Mead aptly described the bottle problem as "the baby on one end and Borden's Dairy on the other."

The rights of mothers came into focus in the forties, when the pendulum swung toward a softer approach. The literature called on a mother to encourage her baby to regulate his own feeding patterns, but at the very same time there was quite a lot of discussion as to whether or not this was good for *her.*

Spock wrote that this freedom might leave inexperienced mothers feeling "uncertain." His audience at this time was mainly the young wives of World War II soldiers who had to spend long periods away from husbands, and who were constantly uprooted and moved to strange locales, sometimes thousands of miles from home and family. So the pendulum reached the other side. A 2-6-10 A.M., 2-6-10 P.M. schedule became the "right" way again.

Underlying this emphasis on scheduling was always the fear (a carry-over from our European and Puritan ancestors) that, given half a chance, the offspring would become too domineering and control his caretaker, rather than learn self-control through discipline.

We had another "thaw" in the early fifties, but a fear that permissiveness might lead to second-rate accomplishments began to haunt us after Russia put her Sputnik into space. The United States saw this accomplishment as a threat and reacted competitively. The Western world believed once more that discipline is equal to and a necessary part of success. The rod was no longer spared!

Vibrations were felt all over. The literature called for a reversion to a more rigid feeding schedule, with recommendations for fewer and shorter periods of nursing, and earlier and faster weaning.

Weaning on Schedule

Weaning patterns have had a similar history, and basically have followed the controls set for feeding. When the time came to wean from breast to bottle or from bottle to cup or from breast to bottle to cup, mothers followed whatever theory (strict or permissive) was popular at the time.

So weaning went through stages of abrupt denial as well as slow and gentle withdrawal, depending on the demands of the period. Over the past seventy years, the time considered proper for weaning has gradually shortened from as much as two or three years to as little as six to eight months (the most frequent time segments suggested at present).

When the term weaning was used, it was mostly meant to describe the change from one method of feeding milk to still another. The very first introduction of solid foods, however, is the true beginning of weaning. At the turn of the century, supplementary foods were supposed to be introduced just before the baby was a year old. During the twenties the recommended time was three to five months. The trend to an earlier age continues. A recent article by Spock suggests it would be all right to start solid foods at one month. The plump baby in food advertisements became the ideal, and many a spoonful of cereal was coaxed into an infant in an attempt to match that image.

Both breast *and* bottle-feeding mothers were subject to all these changing trends. When public opinion switched from baby's needs to mother's rights, both were affected. Whether the milk came through breast or bottle, *all* mothers were asked to tighten or ease schedules. And on the issue of baby's days or mother's nights, mothers of both persuasions were cautioned to spare baby the trauma (and feed him) or themselves the trouble (and not feed him) depending on the prevailing climate.

It's the Fit That Counts

What appears more and more evident is that we must study the baby, whether breast or bottle fed, judge his capacity, note his rhythm and then watch the mother, follow her performance, respond to her preferences, and with this information make up a schedule that fits both.

The bottle gives the mother who is not content only to breast-feed more alternatives. She may choose to use both methods, permitting her some release and her infant some breastfeeding.

Neither breast nor bottle feeding automatically makes a happy baby. What does determine contentment is the choice of the best balance of the many factors involved in his feeding so that both infant and mother are comfortable with the experience.

A Family Affair

By the end of World War II, bottle feeding was the dominant method in America. Ironically, the bottle separated mother from baby, but it brought father and other members of the family closer. Government publications now showed father in photographs accompanying the text. His part in the drama of baby-raising was carefully outlined. His involvement increased with each new edition. Almost simultaneously the infant acquired an older sister and/or brother as well as a decided personality henceforth called "he" instead of "it."

The baby became a family affair. He was removed from the bedroom or nursery (where he had been under the constant surveillance of concerned females) to a place in the sun, bathed in the kitchen sink and propped up in a living room chair.

The bottle widened their living space and made mother and infant less dependent on each other. The mother no longer stayed in bed for weeks, nor did she feel compelled to retire to the bedroom to nurse the baby. Bottle feeding was permitted in full view. Central heating and new drugs made the world a warmer and safer place for both. And, without grandmother to baby-sit, the infant was made more portable so that he could go out with mother.

By giving up breastfeeding and her exclusive hold on the infant, a mother gained a degree of freedom. Father and other members of the family could take over much of the care and feeding of the baby, and the mother focused on outside activities, even a full-time job.

But, at this point, a curious thing happened. As bottle feeding gained wider acceptance, mothers began to worry about whether or not bottle babies were getting enough love and security. They became apprehensive. It was now time to coddle those women who had decided *not* to nurse. Now *they* needed protection against the growing mystique, which claimed that love was possible only through the breast.

Along with permissiveness came the idea that giving, breastfeeding and loving were all equated and anything less was looked at askance. Many were wondering if the rise in cigarette smoking or the increase in crime was related to the lack of breastfeeding during infancy. They were not aware of how unlikely it was for any one trait to cause such a complicated and interconnected change.

Proponents of artificial feeding clamored for reassurance that bottles didn't stand for selfishness. All kinds of efforts were made not to indict the mother or make her feel guilty or inferior. "Love comes from holding and cuddling as much as from mother's milk," she was told.

Within a decade the pendulum swung back once more as the country became more committed militarily. Now the women who need help, protection, and information are those who will breastfeed despite a bottle-oriented world and those who won't accept any other way because it does not complement their new back-to-nature life style.

The most popular baby books today contain a little (but not enough) information on how to manage breastfeeding or what to do in case of trouble. Most American babies by now have inherited grandmothers who themselves were bottle feeders. There's practically no one left who remembers the old urgencies, the old tales and ways.

7

The Breast, Inside and Out

How It All Began

FEEDING YOUNG FROM SOME SORT OF BREAST WITH SOME KIND OF fluid began over 200 million years ago. Primitive mammals were feeding their offspring from a simple breast-like structure while still laying eggs and hatching them. The mammalian characteristic of giving birth to live young didn't evolve until much later. When this combination—live birth *and* lactation—finally came together, it must have had advantages, because it appeared in 18,000 different species of mammals.

Not all of nature's "inventions" worked, however, and inefficient breast structures may easily have contributed to the extinction of thousands of species through the ages. Unfortunately, we shall probably never know since breast tissue, unlike bones, leaves no remains for the physical anthropologist. However, many of these evolutionary "experiments" were successful, and

---

° The most comprehensive work published to date concerning all aspects of lactation is S. K. Kon and A. T. Cowie's two-volume edition entitled *MILK: THE MAMMARY GLAND AND ITS SECRETION* (Academic Press, New York 1961). Most of the information in this and subsequent chapters on lactation was compiled from this source. See also *Lactogenesis*, Monica Reynolds & S. J. Folley (University Pennsylvania Press, 1969); *Lactation*, Ian Falconer, ed. (Butterworths, London 1971).

the end results are the different varieties of breast glands found in today's mammals.

The system of feeding the young directly from the mother's body was a giant step forward. Before this the parents led their young to the sources of food or they carried fruit, seeds and insects back to them. The new method also was the key to the dramatic change in the relationship between mother and young. It was the beginning of truly intimate contact and total dependency.

How do we trace a development which started millions of years ago? In order to find clues as to how different animal structures evolved, scientists often search the brush of Australia. This continent, once attached to the mainland of Asia, broke off after early mammals had appeared but before many of today's species had evolved. This allowed for a separate evolution of many animals, with some interesting deviations.

For instance, the Australian duckbill platypus (*see* illustration), technically a mammal, still lay eggs and hatches them. The mother lies on her back while her young feed by licking a secretion which appears at the ends of long mammary hairs on the front surface of her body (Smith 1959). Some researchers think these simple structures are merely elaborate sweat glands from which the first rudimentary breasts must have evolved.*

The kangaroo shows a more developed milk gland similar to the familiar mammalian breast, but with the unique characteristic of producing two types of milk from two teats for young of different ages. The young kangaroo is born alive but in a very underdeveloped state. With incredible agility, this one-inch immature "joey" climbs up along a track of hair into the mother's pouch. There it remains for several months firmly attached to a raised teat, which it locks in its mouth. A juvenile standing outside the pouch will reach inside and nurse from an elongated teat and receive milk different in quantity and quality from that sucked by the newborn "joey" (Smith 1959). (*see* illustrations.)

---

* For a summary of the theories about the origin of the breast gland see my review (Raphael 1966, pages 82–91).

The opossum, a North American animal, gives us still another variation of this same theme. Immediately after birth, the young clamp onto the teats on the underside of the mother's belly, and she walks about with her progeny swinging below (Smith 1959).

Most species of mammals have complex gland structures like human beings, with a definite nipple from which the animal sucks. In both male and female animals, these glands are technically known as mammae (mamma, when speaking only of one). When speaking of animals one usually refers to udders or teats and to their related structures on human beings as breasts and nipples.

It is a mistake, however, to assume that all animals have mammary glands that are similar to each other but different from human breasts. In reality, there is an enormous variety in the number of glands, their placement on the body, and the design of the internal structure.

The horse, for example, has two mammae, but the hog, also hoofed and four-legged, has as many as eighteen. The horse's teats are placed between the hind legs, yet the elephant's two teats are located on the chest area.

But looks are deceiving. Both horse and cow have one udder. The horse has two separate internal glands leading to the two external teats. The cow's udder contains one large gland which empties into four teats. On the other hand, one wouldn't suppose that the dog, with five paired glands, is at all similar to man. Yet the internal structure in the glands of both, houses many ducts which lead to only one central nipple.

All these variations seem puzzling. But it appears that accessibility and convenience for the young somewhat determines placement. The number of offspring is generally related to the number of teats or nipples. Human beings, for instance, usually give birth to one baby, and two nipples are adequate (even for twins). On the other hand, animals that give birth to litters should have rows of teats, and they do.

How the Breast Develops

A small band of cells, the first rudiments of the human mammary gland, is already visible in the embryo when it is a mere

1/16 of an inch long. Within three weeks, this band becomes a raised area called the "milk line" which extends down both sides of the body in both sexes from the armpit to the inner thigh (Schultze 1892).

The lower end of the milk line disappears in a few weeks, leaving a primitive mammary bud on the upper body. Infrequently, this stage backfires and the individual, male or female, is born with one or more supernumerary nipples anywhere along this line (*see* illustrations). Plastic surgery can eliminate these extra buds, which are usually a source of embarrassment (LaRoe 1947).

These cells develop into a small nodule by the third month. Then nothing much occurs until the fifth month of pregnancy when normally one bud on each side again begins to grow. Fifteen to twenty lobes now form, which will eventually be the center where milk is manufactured in the adult female breast. Toward the end of the mother's pregnancy, ducts appear leading to the newly formed nipple (Raynaud 1961).

In the final stage of development, just before birth, the nipples, which until now have been depressed below the surface, push outward and become level with the skin. In some fetuses, this stage fails and results in the not uncommon partially or completely inverted adult nipple (Raynaud 1961). This does not impair the function of the breasts, as many women fear. With manual help or a nipple shield worn during pregnancy, women with inverted nipples can and do lactate and breastfeed.

Witch's Milk

Between the third and eighteenth day after birth, some infants' breasts become congested and secrete a fluid known popularly as "witch's milk," *lait de sorcière,* or *Hexenmilch* (Mayer & Klein 1961).

This curious phenomenon occurs in both sexes and is thought to be caused by an influx of the mother's sex hormones, which pass through the placenta into the fetus immediately before birth and stimulate this development. Premature infants or those born shortly before term and not exposed to this last-minute surge don't secrete this fluid (Halban 1905).

If this yellowish, colostrum-like, substance is continuously extracted from the infant's breast, it assumes the characteristics of "true milk" and the supply can be prolonged by constant milking. In normal cases, the gland is not manipulated and after twenty days or so the secretion stops (Lorenz 1929).

The Breasts of Children and Adolescents

The breast gland in both boys and girls is made up primarily of a few branching ducts lined by flattened cells and surrounded by connective tissue. While little change occurs throughout childhood, during puberty the reproductive organs, including the breast, show a spurt of development. In response to hormones, the female mammary ducts which were dormant begin to elongate, and cells within these ducts start to develop.

Around the time of the onset of menstruation, a thick layer of fat is deposited under the skin and forms the firm and enlarged adolescent female breast. The areola (the pink skin around the nipple) and the nipple itself also grow and take on a deeper color.

The female breast, even at this partially developed stage, is unique since only human beings develop and maintain permanently protruding breasts. With the exception of a few highly domesticated man-bred animals, like cows; the breasts in all other mammals recede and flatten once suckling stops.

The Breast of the Mature Woman

Each month, during a woman's menstrual period, a surge of hormones stimulates a limited amount of actual growth in the lobes and ducts of the breast gland. As a result of this development and the retention of fluid in the tissue, the breast loses its conical shape and becomes rounder. The change is hardly noticeable in some women, but others gain as much as one-and-one-half pounds per breast each month (Newton 1961).

These changes occur only in the connective tissue, fat, and fluids, while the glandular parts of the breast remain the same unless a woman becomes pregnant. After menstruation, the size and weight diminish, only to begin the cycle again the following month.

Changes During Pregnancy

The most dramatic changes occur during pregnancy. The glands swell and the blood supply increases (*see* illustrations). Many women, in fact, know they are pregnant because of these characteristic signs.

Now nipples become extremely sensitive to the touch and often stiffen or project sometimes with only the slightest irritation from clothing. Veins dilate and can be seen through the skin, now thin and streaked. These dilated blood vessels and accumulated fluids often produce a feeling of pressure.

Sometime during the second or third month of pregnancy, the pink skin around the nipple darkens and becomes brownish. (The areola returns to its lighter shade after nursing stops, or shortly after delivery if the mother doesn't breastfeed.)

The nipple and areola enlarges, as much as doubling in size. A ring may develop around the areola. The surface of this skin appears rough because of the many now enlarged and distended glands beneath it (*see* illustrations). These small but important glands, called *tubercles of Montgomery*, secrete an oily fluid during the breastfeeding period, which protects the skin by lubricating it. Scrubbing, even cleaning the nipple before nursing (which new mothers are often instructed to do) wipes off this natural protection and tends to *cause* rather than prevent nipple damage (Newton 1952).

When the baby is born, the mother's breasts are at their peak of development. The glands are ready to secrete milk even before the birth takes place, but the final process is held in check until approximately the second day (postpartum) by a delicate hormonal balance.

If we stop to think about it, the breast gland does not follow the same developmental pattern as the rest of the body. Most other organs enlarge proportionately as the body grows. Maximum growth of the breast, however, is never reached in the male, nor is it automatically attained in the adult female. Maximum development is brought about only through pregnancy. This peak can occur in a young girl who has not even reached full adult growth or in an adult woman whose reproductive functions are in the declining stages. Unlike other organs, the breast follows its own unique pattern, functioning only as long as the infant sucks, and diminishing in size when the nursing period is over.

The Breast During Menopause

The breast may slightly enlarge at menopause in response to hormonal changes (Newton 1961). If a woman is lactating, she can continue to do so during and after this period. If she is not, however, atrophy begins and the gland shrinks as the amount of ovarian hormones decreases. Should she gain some weight at this stage, the slight decrease is hardly noticeable.

In men, gradual atrophy takes place between the ages of 40 and 55. This process is reversed sometime after 55, when the breasts, responding to hormonal changes, show renewed growth and sometimes appear rather pendulous. From then on the breast remains in a stable condition and no further changes occur.

The Male Breast

Why do men have breasts at all? They certainly have no function. Some clues are found by studying the gland in its earliest stage.

The breast cells in the human male and female start out exactly alike. However, at a very early stage, hormones secreted by the male fetus inhibit the developing breast gland in the *male* embryo (Raynaud 1961).

Since both sexes in all mammals develop breasts, one answer could be that it was simply more efficient for nature to supply the potential for mammary glands in both, and then stop the male breast from developing beyond a certain point.

Some people have speculated that males of some extinct species may have actually fed young from their teats. This theory gains strength from the fact that pregnancy is not essential to lactation. Virgins have been known to lactate (page 69) and on page 92 the whole process by which women nurse adopted babies, even though they were never pregnant, is discussed in detail (*see* footnote° below).

Many have noticed that in the animal kingdom a definite relationship exists between the external appearance of the male and his role in feeding the young. Among some birds, for instance, the sex with the most brilliant plumage does *not* feed or rear the offspring. When the female is more colorfully plumed as with the button quail and the red-necked phalarope, she does the courting, lays the eggs, and then leaves. The male hatches the eggs and tends the young. When the male is splendid with color, like the peacock, he has little to do with egg or offspring. When the male and female tend to look alike as do most shore and song birds, both partners share in the rearing (Etkin 1964).

The human male, responding to his animal heritage, is also comfortable with infants. Despite cultural sanctions that suggest a man's place is elsewhere, fathers quite easily take over the feeding of the young, often with pleasure, as soon as the bottle makes it possible.

If we take an objective look at the human race, both sexes *are* similar in appearance, except for the sex organs and the breasts of females. Men do not have huge protruding jaws or projecting canine teeth, nor are women differently colored or much different in size. Cultural roles and artifacts often confuse maleness and femaleness. These days, long hair styles and even clothing can no longer be used as an easy clue to distinguish sex.

° "Briefly the phenomenon sometimes termed 'non-puerperal induced lactation' has been, and, in some areas, still is, a well-recognized culturally accepted emergency method of feeding young babies whose mothers have died in childbirth. There is considerable literature in anthropological and historical records (Jelliffe 1968; Newton & Newton 1951) and the writers have personally observed induced lactation in various parts of the world, including the Yoruba community of Nigeria, [where] samples of breast milk from [the substitute mothers] were found to show a low normal protein content (Jelliffe 1952).

"Also, lactation induced by sucking stimulation is reported in adult men (Gates, In press), a surprising finding perhaps, until one pauses to reflect that milk production is well recognized in males in the form of neonatal *Hexenmilch*.

"More recently, breast-feeding of adopted children, as noted in Dr. Cohen's letter (*Pediatrics* Dec. 1971:997) has been undertaken successfully by numerous mothers in the U.S.A., Western Europe and Australia following induced lactation (Raphael, 1966; Hormann, 1971)." (Excepts from letter to the editor of *Pediatrics* by Jelliffe & Jelliffe 1972).

The Making of Milk

What's Inside

The breast is not a large muscle. Muscles underly the organ but they have nothing to do with milk production. Breast size and shape are determined by age and the amount of fat around and within it. This fat acts as a shield and plays no nutritional role in lactation. The functional part of the breast is fairly small, containing a network of vessels and sacs, which is protected by these sheaths of fat (Netter 1954).

This exquisitely complex gland might be compared in structure to a river system. Starting from the inside out, thousands of tiny pools empty into hundreds of tributaries which drain into a main river. This river fills a storage reservoir, which in turn empties into a channel leading out to the end of the system. Multiply this one system by 15 or 20 and you have a general picture of the internal gland. *See* illustrations for the actual structure which may help the reader to visualize it.

The Making of Milk°

The areas where the milk is made, stored, and expelled can also be pinpointed on the illustration. Starting from the inside out once again, millions of bits of raw material are brought by the bloodstream to the cells which line the little sacs called *alveoli*. The various components of milk are manufactured in these cells and then secreted into the alveolus sacs and further into the *lumina* or tubes, which drain like the tributaries of a river into storage reservoirs called the *sinus lactiferi* or *ampullae*. There, they are dammed up awaiting release.

It has been estimated that only about 5 percent of all women are physically incapable of some form of lactation (Spence 1938; Deem and McGeorge 1958). Apparently most females can make milk, though certainly not all can deliver the amount necessary to keep an infant alive. Farmers used the term "coffee cow" to describe those animals that couldn't produce much milk. There are certainly human females who are also physically tuned to produce just a small amount. Besides this there are differences in milk content and no doubt some women have milk that is not as nutritious as that of others.

° See my more comprehensive discussion (Raphael 1966, 168–173).

Lastly, there are those mothers and infants who simply don't mesh, physically or emotionally.

But the majority of women can lactate sufficiently. They can produce the milk but there is still that critical question, can they release it. Can they make it available for the infant? This is the next stage in the process and in the majority of cases it determines whether or not breastfeeding will work.

The Let-down Reflex°

When the infant sucks, nerves in the nipple send messages to the pituitary gland in the brain. This triggers the release of a hormone called *oxytocin* into the bloodstream. Within a few seconds, this chemical stimulates the mammary cells around the pools where the milk is being stored, causing them to contract and release the milk.

This is the let-down or *ejection reflex* that propels the milk out of the mammary sinuses and into the central ducts leading to the nipple. If the reflex is strong enough, the milk will shoot right out through the nipple in a constant stream. Artists have pictured this in religious scenes of the Madonna and Child (*see* illustration), and folk myth has used this ejection to explain the creation of the stars in the Milky Way (*see* illustration).

Women describe the sensation of this reflex as strong, tingling and one that gives a sense of "pins and needles." They speak of it mostly as pleasant, though at first startling. Occasionally one hears a woman remark that it makes her uncomfortable.

Experienced mothers clearly understand the relationship between the feeling of "let-down" and the appearance of "true milk." Many feel this sensation throughout the whole nursing period. The sound of the baby's crying or even just thinking about him can cause an immediate release of milk for some (Newton 1958). For other women, the ejection reflex only occurs once the infant starts sucking, and the sensations associated with it are no longer felt after the first few weeks.

But no matter how long or how hard the newborn sucks, and no matter how much milk is stored in the breasts, *it cannot be*

° In my work (Raphael 1966:173–9) I review the history of the discovery of the ejection reflex in cows (Ely & Petersen 1941) and in the human female (Newton & Newton 1948).

drawn out if this reflex is inhibited (Newton & Newton 1958). Simply put, no ejection reflex, no continuing milk secretion. Later on we talk at length about what happens when this reflex is inhibited by an upset mother and how this problem can be avoided.

It's interesting to note that researchers have artificially created the complex hormone, oxytocin. When inhaled by mothers who are able to let down only part of their milk supply, the "locked in" milk is usually released immediately.

Other hormones are also involved in let-down, and we are just beginning to understand their complexity. For instance, different amounts of the same hormone can cause opposite reactions. Estrogen is the hormone which is injected immediately after delivery to stop a mother's milk supply if she is going to bottle feed. Yet this same hormone, when administered in small doses, will enhance the supply.

The hormone that ordinarily holds off lactation until delivery need not affect the woman who is still breastfeeding another child, so pregnancy and lactation can go on simultaneously.

In normal situations, the hormones which control milk secretion circulate in the bloodstream only after childbirth. There is a delicate balance between a decrease in the ovarian hormones and an increase in the pituitary (prolactin) hormones. Abnormal amounts of the same hormones have caused breast "milk" to appear in nutritionally deprived male prisoners of war (Mayer & Klein 1961) and in virgin girls suffering certain pituitary and liver ailments (Deanesley & Parkes 1951). We know, too, that damage to certain nerves can cause fluids to appear, and that some tranquilizers in very large doses enhance lactation (Rahill 1957; Winnick & Tannenbaum 1958).

Besides the ejection reflex, there are other factors upon which success or failure depends. First, the mother's nipple must fit the infant's mouth and encourage him to suck, and second, the baby's sucking must create the vacuum that causes the breasts to refill.

The All-important Nipple

The mother's nipple *must* be long enough to reach the baby's palate, stimulate the throat area, and make him suck. If the nipple isn't long enough or is poorly shaped, the infant will become lethargic and stop trying. This condition, often found in fair-haired Europeans, can be corrected by the use of a nipple shield, which will push the nipple forward and outward (Gunther 1955).

Though most mothers' nipples and babies' mouths are compatible, there is still another problem. The same sort of indifference (which is seen as "rejection" by some mothers) occurs after a baby has choked on and refused a nipple which is *too long*. This problem can easily be corrected by holding the breast in such a way that some of the nipple is withheld from the baby's mouth (Gunther 1955).

An even more common problem is encountered by mothers whose babies are given bottles from birth prior to breastfeeding. Mavis Gunther discovered that the baby who is bottle fed uses a different mouth technique. In fact she can tell how a baby has been fed just by watching him.

"The bottle-receiving mouth technique consists of rounding the lips, expecting the food to come from straight in front, and holding the tongue high and close to the palate. It is as if the baby were guarding against having something thrust too far into his mouth, whereas the baby taking the breast needs to use a small indrawing action to pull the nipple into a widely opened mouth. Once the baby's technique has been adjusted to taking a bottle it becomes much harder to get him to take the breast. . . . Once the baby has become adept at taking the breast, competition from the bottle does not matter; the baby becomes skilled with both (1970, p. 70)."

These are good examples of why mothers should know as much as possible about breastfeeding even before their infants are born. When they don't, these distraught women construe the baby's refusal to suck as their fault, and they suffer a real sense of guilt, never realizing that a structural defect of too short or too long a nipple or too tiny, too broad or too long a mouth could be interfering with the sucking reflex.

Sucking Is Vital

Success also depends on the constant emptying of the breast. The baby's sucking reflex keeps this process going. Milk will come in for a few days after its appearance whether or not the infant is put to breast. After that the gland must be emptied at frequent intervals or the process will be inhibited and less and less milk produced.

What will happen if the milk is left in the breast? It will be reabsorbed. However, if a lactating breast is pumped twenty-four hours after it was last emptied, it yields less milk than it would have after eight hours. Failure to empty the glands creates a pressure within the cells that results in a slowing down of the manufacture of more milk. This is a prime reason why breastfeeding infants *should* be given night feedings.

A complete absence of sucking will cause the gland to recede and lactation to stop. Sucking increases the milk flow in a kind of complementary process between baby and mother's breast.

The Secretions of the Breast

Colostrum, the Mysterious Fluid

Toward the end of pregnancy and for the first few days after birth, the same cells which manufacture milk make and secrete a fluid called *colostrum* (Macy 1949). This substance resembles milk but is thicker. Some scientists believe that colostrum is merely milk that has thickened because it has been stored for a time and reabsorbed in the breast cells.

How this unique fluid is formed and why it is different from milk remains somewhat of a mystery. Certainly it readies the gland for the secretion of "true milk." Its very presence encourages the infant to suck, which not only reinforces the sucking reflex, but prepares the mother's nipples by toughening them.

In only three days or so the chemical content of colostrum changes quite dramatically. The transition though, occurs gradually.

This first fluid contains 10 percent protein, which drops to 2 percent after only eight days. There is also a high concentration of antibodies immediately after birth, which declines rapidly after the first two or three days. Colostrum also contains many enzymes and miscellaneous properties such as estrogens. One curious product is the "cell digesting" cells, which are thought to act as "scavengers" against invading microorganisms within the breast and possibly within the infant gut.

When lactation ends there is often a colostrum-like substance still in the breast. This is often called "regression milk" which is again high in proteins and enzymes and also contains some sugar.

Colostrum is recognized as different from milk in most parts of the world. In the majority of cultures the mother is permitted, even encouraged, to nurse her newborn from the very beginning. Others consider colostrum "unhealthy" for the baby, and mothers are prevented from breastfeeding until their "true milk" appears—somewhere between three and seven days after delivery.

Many societies that are almost exclusively dependent on cattle, ban early breastfeeding. Perhaps human colostrum is mistakenly associated with cow's colostrum, which is much thicker, rather gooey, and often contains spots of blood. To some people this makes it objectionable. (The French, however, prize this cow's substance, sometimes called "early milk," from which they make a special cheese.)

What's in Human Milk?

Almost all we know about the contents of mother's milk we owe to studies of the cow. Funds for research on human milk are almost nonexistent. The kind of experimentation required is also difficult to carry out on human subjects.

What's in human milk? Water, lactose (sugar), fats (cream), and proteins—the same ingredients found in *all* mammary milk (Barry 1957). Looking at the chart (opposite) and comparing the contents of cow and human milk, one might be led to believe that they are almost exactly alike. But this is not so. Though the contents appear similar, we should not be fooled by percentages.

The story is not so simple. Each of the fat globules, for instance, contains thousands of different molecules surrounded by complex membranes. But the molecules in cow and human milk are structurally different. The proteins (containing many types of casein, albumin, globulin, and innumerable whey proteins) are different too.

Like the pieces of a jigsaw puzzle, human milk and the infant's digestive system mesh. On the other hand, while the baby can assimilate enough cow's milk to keep it healthy, many extra "puzzle pieces," resulting from the different molecular structures, just don't fit and are left over. (This accounts for the greater frequency and larger volume of bowel movements in bottle babies.)

Furthermore, because there are so many components in milk, there are innumerable possibilities for differences. For instance, there are many vitamins, minerals, enzymes, phosphates, lipids (butterfat), peptones, nitrogenous bases, and gases, to mention just a few.

Commercial companies making artificial milk now claim that their products are more like mother's milk (implying superiority).

TABLE 1

Comparison of Contents of Cow and Human Milk*

Composition	Human milk	Cow's milk
Water, 100 ml	87.1	87.3
Energy, kcal	75	69
Total solids	12.9	12.7
Protein	1.1	3.3
Fat	4.5	3.7
Lactose (sugars)	6.8	4.8
Ash	0.21	0.72
Proteins, % of total		
Casein	40	82
Whey proteins	60	18
Ash, major components		
Calcium, mg	340	1,250
Phosphorus, mg	140	960
Vitamins per liter		
Vitamin A, IU	1,898	1,025
Thiamin	160	440
Riboflavin	360	1,750
Niacin	1,470	940
Vitamin C, mg	43	11
[Reaction	Alkaline	Acid]

* From Gyorgy, Paul "Biochemical aspects." The American Journal of Clinical Nutrition 24: August 1971, 971.

The base is cow's milk, but the content has been changed in an attempt to duplicate mother's milk as closely as possible.

Actually, the only milk that might be similar to human milk is the milk of the other primates—the apes and monkeys. At the other end of the scale, mammals that live in completely different environments have very different milk contents. For example, the milk of the porpoise, that gentle mammal of the sea, contains 50 percent fat and only 11 percent protein.

One of the few studies done in the early thirties on human beings clearly illustrates the health benefits which can result from good applied research. Scientists found that the strippings (the very last of the milk in the breast at a feeding) contains the highest percentage of fats (Lowenfeld et al, 1934). With this knowledge, weight and digestive problems could be controlled by the length of the nursing period. The infant who needed less fat would be nursed for a shorter period of time at each feeding, while the one who required extra fat would be encouraged to nurse for a longer span.

Much more research of this kind is badly needed.

Now we sift through many fictions and a few factual studies to enlarge the breastfeeding mother's knowledge about her chosen method.

8

Bottle or Breast?

BREASTFED INFANTS ARE NOT MORE STABLE, AND BOTTLE-FED children are not better disciplined. Breast-giving mothers are not necessarily more permissive, nor are their bottle-feeding sisters more eager to toilet train. Many very maternal women choose to bottle feed; yet by the same token some female business executives have been known to rush home during lunch so as not to miss breastfeeding their infants.

Major differences in babies' personalities, which are sometimes attributed to the method of feeding, may, in fact, have been influenced more by the mothers' method of handling the infant. The *manner* in which a mother feeds her young and the infant's response are what matters. The *correct* method for her is the one that fits both partners. Before bottles, a woman had no choice. Now she has a chance to feed whichever way she likes.

By the time a woman reaches adulthood, whether or not she has given the matter any serious thought, the method she will use to feed her infant is pretty much set. She may not know it, but her decision is a result of many factors—her way of life, her choice of friends, her childhood experiences, and her present situation.

Whatever her choice, she must realize that most of her early experience with a newborn infant involves feeding. So the more she knows about this early period, the more confident she will be in her caretaking and the better the baby will thrive.

The Relationship Is the Thing

The importance of this early period was dramatically demonstrated at Cornell University in experiments with goats. When a mother goat was separated from her kid for a period of time shortly after birth, she lost the necessary opportunity to nuzzle, smell, see, and generally identify her kid among all other young in the herd (Blauvelt 1956).

As a result, when the kid was returned to her after only a few hours, she rejected him. If that kid were a female, she might somehow survive and even give birth but she was often so mentally damaged that though she and her offspring were left undisturbed, she was unable to mother her own kid. The researchers had to take over or the newborn animal died.

Human infants are equally vulnerable. They too must be mothered satisfactorily or they wither and die. What is commonly referred to as "maternal instinct" cannot be counted on. A woman can repress maternal feelings and be totally indifferent to her infant. Even the presence of extra hormones in a mother's body is not necessarily enough stimulus to automatically draw her to her child. Yet we know how vital it is for her to establish a deep relationship at this early time.

Doubters will scoff and snap that in great-grandmother's day women managed very well without such theories. However, throughout much of the world, before bottle feeding became safe, it was not unusual for a woman to lose at least her first baby. We know now that one common cause of death was the inability of the mother to work out a relationship and establish a symmetrical rhythm with her child.

Back in 1867, a perceptive French industrialist, horrified at the 40 percent infant mortality rate in his district, decided to do something about it. He offered his women employees a six-week paid vacation immediately after they delivered a baby, so that they could stay home and establish a feeding routine with their newborn infants. The death rate immediately dropped from 40 to 25 percent (*Scientific American* 1867, 1967).

Years ago, even where medical and physical care and sanitary conditions were exemplary, orphaned babies had a high death rate. They seemed to just quietly fade away. The infants who survived often had something special about them, like a mop of curly hair or great big eyes. Luckily for them, these appealing features attracted attention even from busy staff members. The adults would stop, no matter how briefly, and relate to these beguiling infants long enough to make a difference. The infant got a feeling of "self" that made him want to go on living (Spitz 1945, 1946).

As soon as this was discovered, an experimental program of volunteer mothering for one group of institutionalized infants was tested. Each baby was cuddled and tended every day by the same person for a regular period of time. Even when the period was short, the response was astonishing. Babies stopped dying!

Fortunately, nature provides the infant with a few built-in behaviors that appear attractive and encourage response. Such things as the smile that excites adults and the enticing baby smells which cause them to nuzzle, and many other behaviors will be discussed in depth later on.

Close contact between the mother and her infant from the very beginning permits these stimuli to pull them toward each other. The mother learns in these tender moments who her infant is, what he or she likes, how best to keep this tiny person comfortable, and how to enjoy it. All mothers need this vital attachment. The bottle-feeding mother needs early close contact with her infant in order to intensify their relationship. The breastfeeding mother needs it for an additional very important reason. Within this intimate experience she *must* establish the ejection reflex, which as we stated in the last chapter, is vital to continuing the milk flow.

Emotionally, each mother must work with the feeding method most suited to her. Many women, as we mentioned before, are not comfortable with the idea of breastfeeding and should not be forced or even persuaded to try it. But the woman who wants the closeness and involvement that goes with breastfeeding should not be bullied either into changing her mind. We are fortunate that we have reached a point in time where the mother's contentment can come first. Thus, since feeding begins with the mother, she must be permitted the choice which can make her early experience with her baby the most fulfilling.

The Fact of the Matter—$Milk_1$ or $Milk_2$

One of the hottest feeding controversies is over the relative value—or the danger—of the two types of milk. Whether a woman decides on cow's milk or mother's milk, she must feel confident that she is doing right by her infant. The more facts she has, the less vulnerable she will be to the will of others.

As a start, two facts deserve special note. Breastfeeding mothers must remember, in all their excitement, that many of us would be dead if it weren't for bottles, because many mothers and babies just don't fit. (Yes, the horrifying truth in many underdeveloped cultures is that half the babies die. Some from disease and other factors, but others no doubt because of maternal/infant incompatibility.) Bottle-feeding mothers, on their side, must know that breastfeeding does not have a special mystique, that it is *not* the *only* way to confer life and love.

To be a loving parent is the important thing. All the more reason some mothers must breastfeed, because for them nursing answers certain deep-seated creative needs which must be filled so that they can be more responsive parents.

Any attempt to make an accurate comparison of mother's milk and cow's milk is premature. The reason is quite simple. The dairy industry is spending millions of dollars to analyze everything about the cow—from the amino acid and fat molecules in her milk to the kind of music that produces the most contented cows with the highest milk yield. Nothing comparable to this amount of research is being done on human mothers or their milk.

It's not difficult to imagine why. Over fifteen million cows deliver more than 120 billion pounds of dairy products each year in the United States alone. Mother's milk feeds only one small infant and has no commercial value. Obviously dollars for research on human milk are much harder to come by. As a result, we continue to harbor misinformation and to make unfair comparisons.

Those who are pro-bottle declare that mother's milk is incomplete, that it lacks iron, and that it also lacks whatever the mother's diet lacks. Bottle critics on the other hand say that cow's milk contains the wrong proteins, and that no human infant gut should be asked to try to digest them.

Truth exists in both statements, but each side often twists the facts to discredit the other. Take the iron issue. True, mother's milk does not contain iron and it can easily be added to cow's milk. Yet fully breastfed babies do not become anemic. At birth they have a high hemoglobin level in their blood, and there seem to be properties in human milk that slow down the decrease of this level (Finch 1967, 1969). In fact, for yet unknown reasons, despite the addition of iron to their milk, artificially fed babies are more likely to become anemic than infants who are breastfed (Josephs 1958).

Infants, older children and many adults, especially Negroes and orientals who have not had generations of cattle keeping to breed out and weed out those who are allergic, can become very ill by drinking cow's milk. This may occur if the lactase enzyme in their intestines which digests milk is either missing altogether or in too small a quantity to be effective. From adolescence on many individuals become increasingly vulnerable. For them, the ingestion of milk or milk products leads to abdominal bloating, flatulence, or diarrhea (Huang and Bayless 1968).

What about those "wrong" proteins in cow's milk which the breastfeeding protagonists speak of when they quip, "Cow's milk is for calves!" The answer is that the infant system thrives by using whatever it needs from the milk and excreting the rest. This accounts for the daily or twice-daily bowel movements of bottle-fed infants, compared with only one-third to one-half as much excretion in the breastfed baby, who makes full use of most of what he drinks.

Researchers at London University are working on the question of why infants drink so much more cow's milk than they seem to need. The thought currently is that the high percentage of protein in cow's milk makes infants thirsty and causes them to "over-drink" (Blurton-Jones, personal communications, 1972.)

Processed milk is pasteurized, homogenized, and evaporated. It is boiled, cooled, chilled and warmed again. The miracle is that so many infants not only do well on it but do very well indeed.

"Bottle people" are quick to remind us that most babies brought up on cow's milk will also live seventy or eighty years. Unqualified comparisons do both bottle and breast proponents disservice.

The breastfeeding mother often feels that, because her milk looks thin and has a bluish cast, it must be "weak." This is not true. Breast milk is slightly colored and much more translucent than cow's milk and this quality has nothing to do with "weakness."

The bottle-feeding mother does have the advantage of knowing exactly how much milk and how many units of vitamins her infant is consuming. The breastfeeding mother, plagued by the uncertainty of how much milk her baby is actually taking in, allays her doubts by frequently weighing the baby before and after feedings.

However, breastfed infants gain weight slowly and should not be compared to bottle-fed babies. The plump infant does have the advantage of pleasing doting parents, but rapid gain in infancy may not be beneficial. Research suggests that it may be related to a higher risk of coronary disease later in life.

Good Cells and Bad Bacteria

We have already mentioned the bacteria-ingesting cells in colostrum and the antibodies that are found in a far higher concentration than in true milk. They give the newborn immunity to various diseases such as measles, bronchitis, and pneumonia (Stevenson 1947, Douglas 1950), as well as other respiratory infections.

For this reason, some doctors now recommend that even women who prefer using the bottle, breastfeed for a very short time so that the baby will benefit from these early built-in protections. This theory may be further supported by the fact that some intestinal viruses affect infants on cow's milk but not those being breastfed.

Breastfed babies also have a lower incidence of other illnesses and have fewer deaths from them. Enteritis (a disease of the intestines) appears twice as frequently in bottle-fed babies (Douglas 1950, Wolfish 1953).

Breast milk is often recommended as the best therapeutic diet for infants with severe or chronic infection of the digestive tract. Even infantile eczema is less prevalent in breastfed babies.

Many allergies are caused by cow's milk, and some, in fact, such as rashes and intestinal reactions, are not uncommon. Known allergies to breast milk are rare. However, before such reactions can be properly diagnosed, the baby is usually put on cow's milk, so the question of allergy to mother's milk remains unresolved. But evidence is mounting that babies who do not thrive on breast milk are usually suffering the effects of insufficient let-down of the mother's milk rather than an allergy.

Mouth Distortion and Tooth Disease

Some dentists insist that tongue thrusting, perverted swallowing, mouth breathing, lip and finger sucking, malocclusion, and other distortions of the mouth and face muscles can be blamed on bottles and their projecting, unyielding nipples (Picards 1959). Many of them prefer and recommend the stronger sucking required of breast feeding because it enhances the development of facial muscles (Davis et al, 1948).

They further charge that when cow's milk stays in the mouth, as it does when a baby falls asleep sucking his bottle, it creates an environment ideal for the development of bacteria and tooth decay (Fass 1962).

If they are correct, breastfed children will have less tooth decay than those who are bottle fed, because most breast milk comes in and is swallowed within the first five minutes of nursing, and little is left in the mouth when the infant falls asleep. Besides, a drowsy baby lets loose the mother's nipple when sucking stops, because once the milk is drained and nursing slows down, the nipple is no longer rigid.

Still, the bottle-feeding mother often feels that the security of a night bottle for a child who is put to sleep alone is far more important than the risk of a few cavities.

Mouth-Lip-Tongue Tension

Researchers have studied finger and thumb sucking (which appear in almost all mammals and even show up in X-rays of unborn babies) to find out whether they have any relation to feeding methods. They have reported that while finger sucking in human beings is prevalent all over the world, thumb sucking is relatively rare.

Anthropologist Elliott Skinner (1966) found that some orphaned African children who had *not* breastfed sucked their thumbs, while breastfed children in that culture didn't do this. Dr. Margaret Mead (1954), reporting on a survey of other anthropologists' data, found finger sucking but an absence of thumb sucking in every group that was observed. She suggested that these non-Western children probably didn't suck their thumbs, because in addition to being breastfed, right after birth, they were not put on their stomachs so they couldn't get their thumbs into their mouths.

But how about all the Western breastfed babies who still suck their thumbs? This contradiction can be explained by noting that in Western cultures infants are seldom permitted as much sucking as those in other cultures of the world. Also these babies may suck their thumbs because the common practice is not to carry infants as much as they do in other countries but to put them down on their stomachs, allowing them easier and prolonged access to the thumb.

But Dr. Mead's study also suggests that the time a thumb-sucking child spends at the breast in Western cultures is not sufficient to relieve the tension in the mouth-lip-tongue area. Infants apparently *need* a great deal of sucking, whether nutritional or not and regardless of whether they are breast or bottle fed. The breastfeeding mother whose infant sucks his thumb is probably removing him from the breast immediately after he has drained it, instead of allowing him to suck until he is satisfied—a common practice over much of the world.

Bottle-feeding mothers may overcome this lip-tongue tension need in their infants by buying "blind" nipples and making holes in them smaller than those in regular commercial nipples. This lengthens the feeding period and prolongs the sucking. If she prefers, the mother may resort to a pacifier—a practice becoming less repugnant to many.

Some children need a great deal more sucking quite apart from a desire for more milk. Once the mother becomes aware of this need for extra sucking and responds to it by permitting lengthy breast-sucking or by offering a pacifier, she can spare her baby hours of needless fussing.

Breastfeeding and the Mother

Breastfeeding is advantageous to the mother almost before the birth process is completed. Many physicians suggest putting the infant to the breast right after the baby is delivered. When the infant sucks, it causes contractions of the mother's uterus, which quickens the expulsion of the placenta. These muscle spasms serve also to close the uterus after the delivery, lessening the chance of hemorrhage.

This process is vital. In England during the blackouts and bombings of World War II, many women who could not reach the hospital in time to deliver were advised to nurse the newborn *immediately* in order to take advantage of this natural protection.

Nowadays, with new techniques, it is easy to protect the bottle-feeding mother as well. The injection of ergot, which is administered in most U.S. hospitals immediately after the delivery of the placenta, inhibits bleeding.

Breastfeeding also functions as a natural form of birth control by inhibiting ovulation (De Gonzalez 1964, Perez, et al, 1971, Raphael 1971). This is a fact, and not a fiction as often averred. What had not been recognized was that the introduction of supplementary foods for the baby upsets this natural protection. No matter how small the amount of food, the subsequent reduction in breastfeeding is sufficient to stimulate ovulation. The further weaning progresses, the greater the possibility of conception, even though the mother is still nursing.

Another fiction that must be dispelled is that a woman who breastfeeds requires extra food, loses her figure, or is forced to diet on foods she dislikes. The fact of the matter is that the additional pounds a woman gains during pregnancy are a kind of cushion against the nutritional demands placed on her body during the nursing period. These pounds are used up in the course of lactation. The woman who maintains a normal diet loses this added weight, without effort, in the first few months of breastfeeding.

Mothers need 600 extra calories daily at the beginning of lactation. This amount rises to over 1,000 by the end of the third month. The breastfeeding period then can be a time of food indulgence rather than tiresome dieting.

As for all that milk that many adults dislike and the nursing mother is exhorted to drink ("Milk makes milk" is a popular belief), what must be understood is that the real need is for *liquid* —almost any kind. Milk is great because it contains so many proteins, vitamins, etc., but where other foods are easily available, water is fine too.

We mustn't minimize the danger to the nursing mother of not taking good physical care of herself. A team of researchers on lactation claims that this period is the one of "greatest nutritional stress imposed by a physiological process on the human body" (Hytten and Thomson 1961). The body is ready for this, though, under normal conditions. For instance, a woman on a starvation diet *can* deliver a healthy baby and breastfeed it for a time, but the cost to her body is enormous. But, if a normal mother maintains an adequate diet there are no depleting effects. This includes the teeth. Dentists decry the old wives' tale about loosing one tooth for each baby. It is not so, they say. It is the busy woman's neglect of herself and her dental visits that is responsible for any extreme tooth decay.

In our culture, where we are taught that sleep comes in eight or so consecutive night hours, the effect of breaking up one's rest for feedings is distressing and often extremely fatiguing. In other cultures, where people are not so conditioned to sleep in the dark and for one long stretch, they find waking for breastfeedings much less of a chore and a much more natural action. They catch up on their rest during the day.

The word "cancer" occasionally comes up in discussions of breastfeeding. While no definite conclusions have been made yet, the World Health Organization's Committee of Experts (1964) did find that women with children and women who breastfed their children for long periods of time were less prone to the disease.

Breastfeeding and the Infant

Infants, when breastfed, have many advantages. First, they get an immediate response to their hunger cries and have the skin contact and body movement from their mothers. Then, they can have additional sucking if they need it. And of course there are the antibodies against disease and allergies.

When breastfed, the infant is assured of time—often extra time—with his mother especially just after birth. An infection crisis in a hospital nursery may mean separation for the bottle baby, but for the breastfeeder, it could mean a special rooming-in arrangement and full-time together.

Infants benefit in other ways too. Only by breastfeeding can a mother be sure that she will be allowed to stay in the hospital with her baby if hospitalization is necessary. Mothers who participated in sit-in or sit-down demonstrations learned this too. Breastfeeding was the only justification the police would accept for keeping a baby with the mother who was jailed.

A Matter of Convenience

Is breast or bottle feeding more "convenient"? The answer must come from the mother.

Time had little to do with convenience in the mind of one nursing mother. "I have nowhere I'd rather be," she responded when questioned about being "tied down."

To one woman it will be convenient to go through the arduous routine of sterilizing bottles and nipples, making the formula, and reheating the milk. At night she will rise from a sound sleep, warm the iced milk, test and adjust it, and keep the baby from waking the family while doing this. But all this will seem convenient to *her* if it insures her the opportunity to come and go as she pleases during the day.

A woman of another temperament will prefer to tuck the baby into her warm bed, put him immediately to breast, finish the feeding, turn over and go back to sleep.

A point of interest here is that babies drinking cow's milk can give up night feedings much sooner than those on mother's milk. The richness and quantity of cow's milk can be adjusted so that an infant can sleep comfortably through the night. The breastfed infant usually receives less milk at each feeding and may need to be fed more often. The breastfeeding mother needs frequent stimulation, so nursing during the night works out well for her.

An important criticism of *only* breastfeeding is that if the mother becomes ill or must be absent, even for a few hours, the infant will starve. The infrequent bottle is said to be an insurance against this danger. Seldom, however, does this happen. When it does, though, there is no question of starvation with bottles available. A baby may fuss and reject this new object at first but never for long. Hunger quickly forces an infant to learn to suck from the bottle. Preference and habit are usually not a problem until an infant is ready for weaning. The difficulty some mothers have experienced during this period tends to make them apprehensive about any supplementary bottles.

Protection for the Breastfeeding Mother

In the long run, we see that both bottle- and breastfed babies get on very well. But what about their mothers? Attitude changes that continue to swing back and forth are common in society. One day sex is out, the next it's table conversation. One day it's all right to strike your child, the next it's against the rule. So it is with feeding methods.

Early in the century, the women who wanted so desperately to be "free" and to use bottles for their infants were denounced as selfish and cruel. Today, the changeover is complete. Bottles are here to stay and we have "liberated" ourselves. But, in doing so, we have insulated ourselves from our own femininity. We no longer feel feminine simply because we have babies. Men cannot get pregnant or carry babies, of course, but ask any mother who delivered her baby and she will tell you her doctor did, or a nurse, or a taxi-driver, but seldom will she answer that *she* did.

Ask her when she intends to wean and she will quote Dr. Spock.

Attitudes toward the breastfeeding mother must be changed. She needs a special kind of separation; she needs indulgence; she needs support. Her feeding choice may stem from a normal feeling that breastfeeding is the only way. Or, her decision may grow out of a number of real deep-seated ego needs, which she may satisfy more easily while breastfeeding than at any other time in her life.

The odds in our culture today are stacked heavily against successful breastfeeding, and the emotional price for failure is high. When a woman fails, she may lose a sense of her true feminine self as well as a treasured experience.

A more serious loss is the mother's confidence in the fact that she is doing the best she can for her infant. Most mothers who want to breastfeed believe that it is the best way and much of their motivation stems from this belief. Defeat means doubts and questions about their maternal competence.

In order to give the reader some idea of how persistence pays off, I next describe a very unique instance of breastfeeding. I use this example to dramatize the fact that breastfeeding is possible despite the most difficult circumstances. These very special cases involve women who breastfeed adopted infants.

9

Breastfeeding the Adopted Baby

"WHAT EVERY ADOPTING PARENT DREADS FINALLY HAPPENED TO me," said Mrs. Turno, a mother of three adopted children. "Andy came in one day sobbing, 'Gregie says you don't own me. You never borned me.' You can't imagine my triumph when I could counter with, 'No, darling, I didn't borned you but I breastfed you!' "

There are many such extra dividends for the increasing number of mothers who are breastfeeding their adopted children.

This doesn't mean wet nursing. Wet nursing occurs when a mother breastfeeds an infant she has not borne, in place of or concurrently with her own infant. It is not an uncommon practice, particularly in the upper-class of many cultures.

Breastfeeding adopted infants is different. Officially called *non-puerperal lactation*, it means the nursing of an infant by a woman who is establishing (first time) or reestablishing a milk supply *without pregnancy and delivery*. The mother may not have been pregnant for years. In fact, there is evidence that even women who have never been pregnant can lactate and nurse an infant. (See Jelliffe's statement on page 66 fn.)

This kind of stimulation of the milk supply apart from the normal reproductive cycle is called *galactogenesis,* meaning the beginning of the lactation process. The term is also used to describe aberrant situations mentioned earlier, of virgins and prisoners of war, where the secretion of breast fluids is a result of disease or malnutrition.

How can this strange phenomenon be explained? One way is by seeing it as a parallel pattern to other more familiar bodily processes. For example, many of the viruses that cause disease as well as the antibodies which produce their cure are always present in the body. They lie dormant most of the time. The point at which they become active depends on exposure, stress, and many other complex factors. Likewise, the potential network of the hormones and tissues involved in the production and secretion of mammary fluids is present in the human body at birth. For example, the rudimentary tissues of the breast and the endocrine glands which produce the lacteal hormones are also present in both sexes at birth.

The real question is what are the metabolic processes and the hormonal balances which keep the milk producing functions *in check?* Under normal circumstances the infant breast at birth can and often does secrete fluids. If the gland is manually milked, the flow will continue. If not, after a few weeks the factors which inhibit milk production take over. The same goes for the growth of the gland and for the presence of lactation in women. Until the inhibitory factors are removed, development at puberty and during pregnancy, and milk production after childbirth does not occur.

Similarly, in regard to nursing the adopted baby this inhibition/release process begins with the stimulation the mother receives from the infant's sucking. In many cases, this alone is sufficient to initiate the appearance of fluids to appear in the breasts independent of the usual sequence of pregnancy and childbirth.

Sure It's True

Margaret Mead described adoption and non-puerperal lactation nearly forty years ago. The Mundugumor of New Guinea, she writes, believe that ". . . the breasts of some but not all (non-lactating) women will secrete milk under the stimulating effect of a child's sucking, combined with drinking large quantities of coconut milk" (1935). While studying these people, she personally tested the weight and growth of two sets of twins, one of each breastfed by his own mother and the other by the adopting mother (grandmother) whose milk supply had been re-stimulated. She found all four had similar growth patterns and good health.

Most people in this country, including physicians, are amazed when told it is possible to bring on the milk supply apart from normal pregnancy. But it is no surprise in other areas of the world. Recently, an Indian obstetrician asked me whether American women had a harder time reestablishing their milk than Indian women. I had to admit that they do.

It isn't that American women are physically different or deficient. They either don't know it can be done so they don't try, or they are in an environment which is unsupportive, even hostile, and they become discouraged early.

In this country, women flounder when attempting to breastfeed even their natural children, much less adopted ones. The reason is that we've forgotten how to deal with even the simplest breastfeeding practices that every girl of ten knew just a few generations ago. But things are changing. We're relearning many of the basic mothering techniques we thought we could do without, part of which include new methods in the art of breastfeeding the adopted child.

Forty Special Mothers

My sources of information about breastfeeding the adopted come from answers I received to a questionnaire I sent to forty mothers who had tried it. What a responsive set of women they were! Proud of their accomplishments and eager to share their experiences, they were an ideal group for any researcher. Many had kept very sensitive and comprehensive diaries of their trials and joys . . . up to eight single-spaced pages which they had mimeographed for other mothers who wrote for help.

Their records were filled with helpful information, encouragement, fear, panic, and testimonials of joy.

Most of these women were at different stages in their reproductive lives when they received their adopted infants and began nursing. The results reflected this diversity. Those who were breastfeeding at the time simply switched babies and went nonstop into their new pattern. In one case, the mother was sure she had not really been producing any milk for her two-year old for months, yet when the newborn adopted infant began sucking, the supply came back very quickly.

Human mothers don't function like the kangaroo we mentioned earlier, but those who begin to feed an adopted child only a few months after weaning a "natural" child are usually successful in a very short period of time. Several babies in this group never had a bottle.

Another set of mothers who had borne natural children and breastfed them in the past, but not at the time of adoption, had to restimulate their supply. After their adopted infants sucked at the breast, they would bottle feed. Often, the child was completely breastfeeding within two or three months.

Those who took longer at getting their supply started claimed they didn't mind the additional chore of bottles. Many discontinued supplementary milk after four to six months but added solid foods to the diet.

A small group of mothers who had never breastfed, but had delivered other infants or had had miscarriages, experienced enlargement of the breasts and produced varying quantities of fluid. The interesting thing about this group is that they had gone through most of the normal hormonal patterns at some time, and as might be expected, were slightly more successful at producing these fluids than those mothers who had never been pregnant and yet suckled adopted children.

The latter group is the best example of the variety of experience and meaning that breastfeeding has in different contexts and with different women. In village India, breastfeeding means first and foremost the infant's survival. In a Western city it means a great deal to the mother and food for the baby. To the adopting couple, the experience of intimacy and closeness takes primacy over the amount of breast milk initially or ultimately stimulated.

92

Who Were These Women?

Were they special? Yes, in some ways. They were a determined lot. They were white, middle-class wives whose husbands had good jobs as insurance brokers, lawyers, real estate agents, university administrators, and the like. They had an average of two years of college and were articulate, self-confident and much older when they adopted than the majority of American women during their childbearing period. Most of them were in their thirties. The youngest was 25 at the time she breastfed and the oldest was 42.

The average family in this small group had two or three children. Some were their natural children.

The mothers stated that their main reason for adopting was that they could not produce more children of their own. A few, however, felt that they had already had their share (two) and were morally bound to care for the surplus children of the world. Some "just had to have little people around." None inherited their infants from relatives or knew the natural mother. All had obtained their babies from state or religious agencies or privately through a lawyer or doctor.

As a group, these mothers seemed to have in common a willingness to take a chance and to expend time and energy first by adopting a baby, and second by attempting to breastfeed. They were highly motivated and determined to make it work.

Their letters and responses to the questionnaires did not indicate unusually dominant personalities. Some described themselves as quite shy. The tone of the letters and responses were gentle. But when it came to breastfeeding their new babies, they gave it their very best try. They were emotional to the point where they could verbalize their doubts, but they also could control their fears, accept offers of help, sing of their victories, and express their gratitude.

Preparing the Breasts

Almost all the mothers "prepared" their breasts in some way before the infant arrived, usually by "massaging" them. How this was done and how often or for what length of time was too difficult to ascertain by written description so I hesitate to suggest that it is a "must."

However, two women who noted a few drops of white fluid during this preparation were so encouraged they recommended preadoption massage above all else for the psychological as well as the physical benefits.

The mothers who used massage or hand pumps were concentrating on getting the milk flow started. Others focused on toughening the nipples, expecting the milk supply would take care of itself if they could avoid the discomfort of cracking and chafing.

Two mothers who were still breastfeeding their natural children were surprised to find that the new infant made their nipples very sore. Apparently different infants have different force behind their sucking, perhaps even a different lip-muscle movement. A more intense nursing rhythm may affect some mothers no matter how long they have been feeding.

One mother who wished she weren't such an expert on the subject of sore nipples suggested that a new baby's more frequent nursings are tougher on nipple tissue than the more vigorous but less frequent sucking of an older child. "Besides," she wrote, "it only hurts for the first few minutes. If you can survive that, your session will go along beautifully."

Several mothers who knew approximately when their adopted babies were to arrive, "borrowed" infants from other mothers, hoping that these experienced suckers would ready their breasts and perhaps even bring on the milk supply. For most, the attempt was too short to be effective. But it did give them the opportunity to acquire some experience with babies, and, more important, it often established a strong supportive relationship with the mothers of the borrowed babies.

What About the Babies?

Two of the infants were of interracial parentage—a mixture of white and Negro, and white and Burmese. The rest were Caucasian. All were healthy, although several had severe allergic reactions to cow's milk (which was discovered once volunteered breast milk or the milk from the adopting mother was discontinued). When such allergies became apparent, frozen breast milk, soybean milk or, occasionally, goat's milk was substituted.

The babies arrived at the adopting parents' homes at various ages ranging from two and a half days to six weeks, with an average of about 20 days. It was generally agreed that the best time to begin the sucking process for maximum results was as early as possible. The younger the baby, the better for the mother. Short frequent nursings from the newborn are best for stimulating the milk supply.

The amount of time the infant sucks and the force of that sucking seem to be critical. Those infants who were lackadaisical never got their mothers' supply up to par. The over-energetic ones that needed a great deal of sucking often irritated the nipples, making the mother uncomfortable. The ideal infant is one who demands only enough nursings to stimulate the mother's milk supply sufficiently. A more demanding one would tend to upset the mother and start her worrying about whether or not she had enough milk.

The Essentials

What did the mothers find most important for making this experiment work?

"The only requirement I will demand from the agency next time," quipped a woman from Arizona, "is a baby that wants to latch on and stay there."

A cooperative baby was a great help to success. Differences in the babies' desire and ability to suck had to balance with their mothers' toughness of skin and need for stimulation.

"He was a gentle sucker." "She was hard to keep at it." "I had a barracuda-type baby," were some of the descriptions mothers gave of their infants.

Variation was the rule. No two babies were described as performing similarly, not even for the same mother. Having breastfed one infant most successfully, one woman who called herself a "careful housewife and creative mother" was very aware of a striking difference in a second, adopted child: "With Oscar it was different. I never did get my supply going strong enough. He just seemed lazy, and never all that hungry."

"The reason I was so successful," said a 35-year-old teacher, "was that I took off a whole semester and just cuddled up in bed with my daughter, read, and nursed her every few hours for several weeks."

There was unanimous agreement that *the major stimulus for bringing on and maintaining the milk was the infant's sucking.* When nursings were reduced, the supplements had to be increased.

A few mothers used the "Buccal Pitocin" nasal inhalator which contained an extract of oxytocin, the hormone that induces let-down through the ejection reflex. That critical key reflex is as important in this special case as it is in breastfeeding which follows childbirth. The reader will remember that when the infant sucks, the pituitary gland releases oxytocin into the bloodstream, causing the cells within the breast to contract and empty the stored milk into the main ducts, where it becomes available to the suckling infant. This goes for breastfeeding natural or adopted children.

The feelings of let-down—that tingling sensation described by women as "a drawing feeling" or "pins and needles"—was often felt very shortly after the baby began to nurse. Apparently the ejection reflex can be experienced before there is any sign of milk. In fact, it can come as an immediate reaction to massaging or hand pumping the breasts even *before* the baby arrives!

This doesn't surprise the breastfeeding pros. They know that the ejection reflex can be felt years after weaning. "I was watching an old family movie," reports a 46-year-old grandmother. "There was my baby son, Jamie, tugging at my blouse to be nursed. The sight made me feel so nostalgic. I was also amused to note that I actually experienced a feeling of let-down in my breasts."

"Rest" was often stated as essential because the caretaking and the constant nursing that was required took so much time. "If you have anything better to do," said the youngest of our informants, "don't bother to breastfeed. You can't do much else for at least 5 or 6 weeks."

Most women agreed that diet was important, but they were not specific as to what foods it should include. Americans are

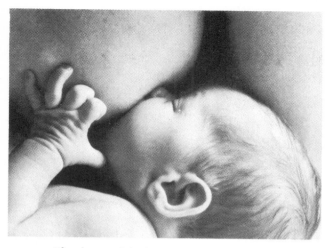

The nursing baby has inspired generations of artists to represent breastfeeding in many real and symbolic forms.

The photograph by Ken Heyman expresses the form and tenderness which the mother-infant scene represents for the 20th-century artist.

"Madonna and Child," School of Soria, Spanish, ca. 1450. This nursing Madonna of the Middle Ages presents the Queen of Heaven as formal, distant and detached from the earthly bodily functions. (Courtesy of North Carolina Museum of Art.)

"Venus, Mars and Cupid," Peter Paul Rubens (1577–1640). The artist uses the breastfeeding pair to symbolize love and mothering but only as an adjunct, an excuse to paint the nude body in a manner expressing the exuberance for life, which was the climate of this period. (By permission of the Governors of Dulwich College Picture Gallery, London.)

"Origin of the Milky Way," Tintoretto (1518–1594). During this era, allegory was a technique frequently used by artists. Here the Master uses lactation to express creation. This painting depicts the Roman mythological story of how Jupiter held his son Hercules to Juno's breast and how her spilt milk (looking very much like a milk ejection reflex) turned to stars. (Courtesy of The National Gallery, London.)

Statue of Artemis from Ephesus, Izmir, Turkey. The mother-goddess theme is epitomized in this symbolic representation of mothering, breastfeeding, fertility, growth, life. (Courtesy Turkish Tourism and Information Office, New York.)

Detail of "Peace and War," Peter Paul Rubens (1577–1640). Here breast-feeding is used to highlight a political statement. Rubens presented this painting to the king as a pictorial expression of those aims for which he worked. War is banished and the children cluster around the rich and plenty of Peace. Peace, the nursing mother, generously contributes her own milk to the feast. (Courtesy of The National Gallery, London.)

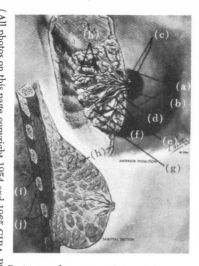

Position and structure of the adult female breast. Showing (a) areola and nipple, (b) Montgomery's gland, (c) 15–20 lactiferous ducts, (d) sinus lactiferi or ampullae, (e) mammary ducts, (f) secondary tubules, (g) lobules or acinar structures with alveoli sacs and milk secreting cells, (h) fat, (i) muscle, (j) ribs.

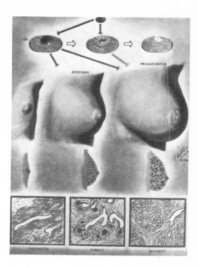

Development of the breast from childhood to maturity showing the effect of the follicle-stimulating hormone and of an increased output of estrogenic hormone on growth during puberty. Also shown is the formation of the corpus luteum which secretes progesterone, promoting further growth of the lobular buds to produce the mature adult female breast.

Progressive development and change during pregnancy and lactation due to a complex interrelationship of hormones and the stimulation from the baby's sucking.

Anomalies of the breast, including hypertrophy of one breast and supernumerary nipples and breast structures occurring along the milk lines.

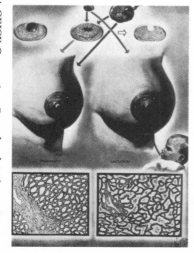

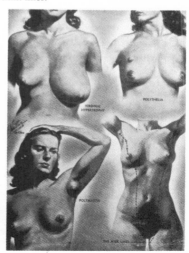

The duckbill platypus, a monotreme, one of the most primitive mammals, is shown in this line-drawing "nursing" three young. The mammary glands are extremely simple, consisting of sacs which empty into a porelike depression. The structure has no nipple. The female platypus feeds by lying on her back and allowing her young to lick the milk that exudes from the glands on her abdominal hairs. The feeding method in this animal has led many investigators to hypothesize that the mammary gland may have originated in this simple way and is in effect, little more than a well-developed sweat gland. (Original line drawing by Simon Greco.)

Left. Newborn red kangaroo on teat in the pouch of its mother. (Courtesy Ederic Slater, CSIRO Australia.)

Bottom left. 50-day-old red kangaroo on teat within mother's pouch. (Courtesy Ederic Slater, CSIRO Australia.)

Below. Newborn red kangaroo on teat within the pouch. Also showing is an elongated teat which is being used simultaneously by an "older" offspring standing outside of the pouch. (Courtesy Ederic Slater, CSIRO Australia.)

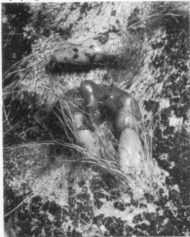

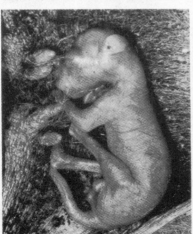

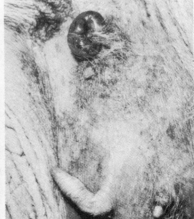

Left. Breastfeeding rituals are probably older than Neanderthal woman. The famed Venus of Willendorf statuette shown here was more likely a lactation amulet rather than the general fertility symbol it was first thought to be.

Below left. The coiffeur of the Venus of Willendorf (dated between 25,000 and 30,000 years B.C.) remarkably resembles a mammary areola when seen head-on.

Below. This presumptive "rubbing" stone was found in a burial area of the Turner-Look Site in East Central Utah. The site was occupied by the Fremont Indians until A.D. 1150. When the stone is held next to a human female nipple of a post-partum multipara, the resemblance leaves little doubt as to the stone carver's subject matter. It was probably used as an amulet with the intent of increasing the milk supply.

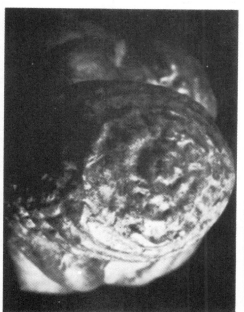

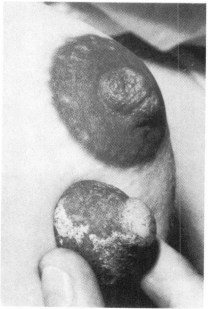

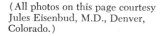

(All photos on this page courtesy Jules Eisenbud, M.D., Denver, Colorado.)

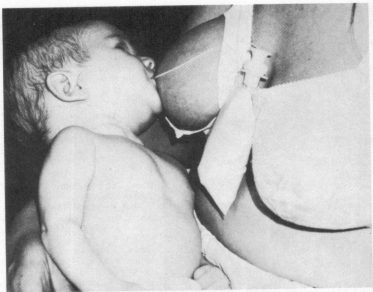

Lact-Aid Nursing Supplementer invented by John Avery of Denver, Colorado, in response to his wife's need to keep their adopted infant sucking while the milk supply was being reestablished. This supplementing nurser releases milk as the baby sucks. It is now used also in cases of severe milk allergy, for stimulating lactation and building up milk supply in those mothers who need help breastfeeding their natural infants, in supplementing a milk supply for the mother of twins, and for reestablishing a nursing relationship after separation of mother and baby due to surgery. (Photograph courtesy J. J. Avery, Inc.)

Moderate protein-calorie malnutrition (PCM) in two-year-old Uganda child displaced from his mother's breast by a new baby. Diseases such as marasmus and kwashiorkor often develop from malnutrition of this type. (Photograph courtesy Derrick Jelliffe, M.D., Caribbean Food and Nutrition Institute, Jamaica, BWI.)

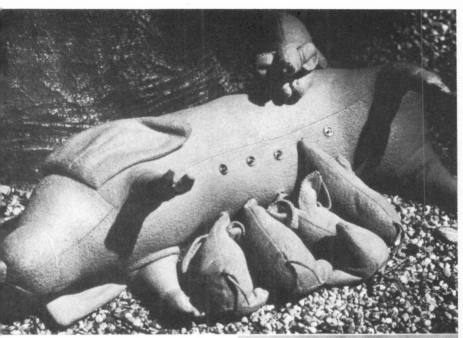

Stuffed pig with five piglets which
snap on to one of ten "snap-on" teats.
This animal was made in Appalachia
and is part of a trend to make
children aware that milk comes from
breasts or teats and not only
from the supermarket. (Photograph
courtesy Seth Jacobson.)

Stuffed doll (made in Uppsala,
Sweden, by Maria Fichtelius) which
"delivers" twins and "breastfeeds"
them with a snap-on mouth
arrangement on the babies which
clasps onto the breasts. It is a far
more subtle method of teaching young
children the "facts-of-life" than the
formal demonstration dolls used in
schools. (Photograph courtesy
M. Fichtelius.)

Muslim mother in India nursing her four-year-old. (Photograph from the Family of Man collection, courtesy Gitel Steed, New York City.)

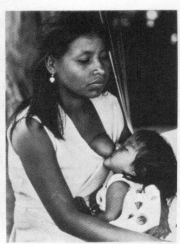

Tikuna mother from a village near the Amazon River nurses her infant. The photo emphasizes one of the many inconsistencies about breast-feeding in emerging cultures influenced by Western patterns. Though women are urged to breastfeed, they are also discouraged in subtle ways; in this case by a blouse which fastens in the back. (Photograph courtesy Trudy Karr.)

A Turkmen mother pauses from her many chores to suckle her youngest in the quiet of her family's yurt (tent). Traditional clothes take into account the needs of mothers to breastfeed their infants at all times of day or night and under all circumstances. In cultures where modesty is required, blouses, head-coverings, shawls, saris, and blankets are all a part of an integrated pattern of work, child-care, and attractiveness. (Photograph courtesy William Irons, Baltimore, Maryland.)

casual about diet and tend to believe that everyone has a normal, adequate eating pattern similar to their own.

Brewer's yeast was praised by almost everyone, though, of course, it is not a magic pill. Eating this fungus doesn't automatically produce milk, but it is an excellent source of vitamins B and G.

Years ago women were saying that beer helped to make milk. Now this prescription is not so common. One mother frankly admitted that she tried anything anyone recommended that wasn't poisonous.

"You name it," she said, "and I'll eat it." She claimed to have no favorites. "The variety of good things I ate," she added, "made me feel I must be the healthiest human mother on earth. I read somewhere that some groups use live larva to increase their milk. Luckily, Jamie was weaned by then."

Indeed, women in many primitive cultures recommend different parts of animals, liquids of various sorts as well as roots or extracts from the bark of special trees or plants. We dare not scoff at these natural substances, for they may really enhance the milk supply. We have learned from the "rediscovery" of the Indian drug, *Rauwolfia* (our Miltown tranquilizers) that some natural substances previously unknown to us are indeed effective. Along with these recommendations, however, goes the edict that breastfeeders must drink, drink, especially water. Fluids are of the utmost importance.

None of the women mentioned using birth control pills while they were nursing. Although we know that full breastfeeding (no supplements whatsoever) does offer a natural form of birth control for a period of time after childbirth (*see* page 83), we don't know if this occurs when milk is reestablished.

"Read everything you can on breastfeeding," recommended one woman from Washington state. "You get courage simply by an awareness that it has been done." Using the La Leche League as their source, several mothers made contact with those relactating alumnae, who generously reaffirmed that it was indeed worthwhile.

"Self-confidence," writes one mother, "is so important. There were so many negative and hostile people, I found I needed self-assurance and a gut-level determination every day to continue doing something so different."

The Physical Side

Though several physicians predicted trouble, breast complications were minimal. A few mothers complained of "plugged ducts" but they successfully "massaged away the clogged milk."

The major complaint was sore nipples. One winter a La Leche League worker reported receiving many calls from mothers with sore nipples all about the same time. How much was coincidence and how much a result of weather and other environmental factors is the kind of information we have yet to discover.

The abundance of milk varied at different times and under special circumstances. One mother noted that her supply lessened dramatically during her menstrual periods. Another commented that her periods were normal for the first time in ten years. One noticed that antihistamines taken for a sinus condition "definitely reduced my supply."

"I was going great, my breasts were developing in response to Janni's sucking until she started sleeping through the night at six weeks and I reduced the nursings from six or seven per day to five. This was a terrible mistake. I noticed a decrease in my breast size within a week."

There were some other effects. "Once I started to feel letdown I became depressed for a few days," wrote one mother. "Like baby blues without the delivery."

One woman who described herself as "five feet one and skinny" said, "For the first time since I was a pimply adolescent, my skin cleared up!"

Most mothers made a very firm effort not to use medicines during their breastfeeding episode. "Not even one aspirin," said an adamant mother. Overcaution seemed to make them more comfortable.

How Was The Supplementary Milk Given?

Sheer ingenuity is the best way to describe how these mothers got supplementary food into their infants. The problem, of course, was to avoid getting the baby used to drinking milk from an "easier" source. Mothers had to find methods to keep the infant sucking despite an empty breast.

Years ago when women asked Margaret Mead about breast-feeding their adopted infants, she usually discouraged them because it meant that the baby would have to be kept a little bit hungry as an incentive for him to suck long enough to stimulate the mother's milk supply. This is what women had to do in the New Guinea cultures she studied. Now that we know a little more about the different types of adopting women—some who start from scratch and use alternatives, others who have at least a trickle of milk, and those who can expect immediate results—we can compensate by balancing sucking and supplement and eliminate the rather unthinkable prospect of deliberately keeping the infant hungry.

One of the alternative methods is to give the infant the bottle before putting him to breast. If he is the type who needs lots of sucking, it works well. If the baby stops sucking as soon as his stomach is full, however, he needs the reverse process—mother's breast first and, when he's really hungry, his fill of cow's milk.

Still a third alternative is to feed a little from the bottle, then offer the breast, going back again to the bottle when the infant becomes restless.

Droppers, spoons, syringes and tubes of many varieties were tried. One father invented a feeder which releases milk as the infant sucks on the nipple. (*see* illustration.) Food is offered in these containers between the baby's lips or in the corner of his mouth while he is nursing. This entices him to continue sucking, gives his mother the necessary stimulation to enhance her milk supply and fills him up besides.

"You have to be careful," laughed one mother who used an eyedropper. "These infants are shrewd. Karen learned how to suck the milk out of the syringe from the side of her mouth and wasn't drawing on me at all. I had to move the dropper nearer the center."

The Crux of the Matter. . . . How Much Milk?

Nursing mothers, as we have mentioned, have long tested the amount of breast milk by weighing their babies before and after feedings (often and unnecessarily—to the detriment of their peace-of-mind). Some of those in our study used this method, while others only approximated the amount they were producing by recording how much or how little supplementary milk the infant was taking. Many kept meticulous records or remembered every detail of increases or decreases in their supply as the infants' needs changed. The records were sources of encouragement and served as a constant check on the baby's condition.

We are at the very beginning. Someday we will have more accurate measures. We will have simple tests to determine the contents and quantity of mothers' milk. Even now, breast fluids, especially colostrum, are being tested at a hospital in Boston—an encouraging sign that researchers are becoming interested.

We can expect that soon new techniques will take out all the guesswork and with it the fears, doubts and uncertainties. But until then we must be satisfied with approximations.

The estimates of milk yield from the group of women who had never been pregnant were the lowest of all—an expected pattern. Most of these mothers experienced let-down and all of them noted some breast fluids. Many were able to express the substance and described it as "milky." In one case a mother said it looked "different after four weeks from the clear fluid I saw at first." The earliest that any fluid was hand expressed was fifteen days after the infant started to suck. The rest had to wait longer. Still, most reported they wouldn't have missed the experience for the world.

"I was sure I had some milk because Glenn was so hungry he wouldn't have allowed any fooling around. I nursed both sides, and when he wasn't getting any more, he'd fuss and demand the bottle."

"I have no idea how much milk I had but I do know I felt full until Jeannie nursed and much softer and empty after. I used a dropper at the same time, so it didn't make any difference. I would have loved having no 'extras' but I enjoyed it anyway."

"I would guess that my baby received about one-third of his daily supply from me. At the highest point of my lactating, he might have had a bit more."

One mother learned quite by accident that her adopted son

was getting fluids from her. She began suffering suddenly from acute attacks of gastritis and at the same time noted that her infant also was full of air which he expelled through the rectum. She discovered after two weeks of discomfort that the non-caloric sweets she was eating all day to hold her weight down contained a substance that was creating the gastritis. She stopped immediately and found that the discomfort ceased—for both.

There were other signs indicating that infants were getting nutrition from their mothers. The experienced breastfeeder knew the light yellowish bowel movements of the breastfed baby. She determined what percentage òf breast milk her infant was receiving and at which feedings by noting the color and texture of each bowel movement.

As one mother reported, "Janet would usually have one stool that was completely from the breast and then several others either mixed or completely from the formula."

The best criterion, of course, was the reduction of formula. One mother who hadn't breastfed in five years cheered, "Debbie was only two months old when I threw away all the bottles."

Who Cares?

Those who are not directly involved often debate the pros and cons of breastfeeding with authority, believing they are neutral on the subject. Often they harbor varying degrees of disapproval. There are also well-wishers who caution too loudly in the guise of honest concern.

Questions about weight, color and health, in general, are especially unnerving. "He really looks pale, are you sure he is getting enough of everything?" or, "If I were you I would weigh him more often." Or, "How do you know what she is drinking is really any good?"

And the jokes. "Well, I believe in the immaculate conception of Our Lord so I guess you can believe in nursing an adopted baby." Or, "Have the Borden milk people heard about you?" Or, "I can believe it, but then I'm one of those people who say that the TV show about our landing on the moon was real!"

Someone must stand between the mother and this not-always-subtle harassment.

It's natural to be curious, even amazed about such an experience. It isn't every day that people learn a completely new fact about their bodies. But thoughtless remarks can be devastating.

"No one asks a mother who has just given birth if she seriously intends to keep her child alive," said one rather angry woman, who just wasn't going to let other people bother her. "Why should anyone ask me? Imagine thinking I would be so egotistical or stupid as to harm my own baby!"

There is so little precedent for this process that it is no surprise that mothers are prone to doubt. Unlike a natural breastfeeding situation, each mother knows from the start that supplementary foods are essential in the beginning and perhaps for the duration of their nursing experience. The question is *how much* supplement should be *withdrawn* or *added* and *when?*°

"It was often scary," said one usually very quiet woman. "Even though I was supplementing my nursing, I worried at times that I might be harming the baby or starving him because so many people asked me that dumb question. I can't tell you how great it felt when my husband would start swearing at their nonsense. He was the most reassuring person."

Most husbands were supportive. The idea of stimulating or restimulating the milk flow was interesting to them and they were creative with helpful innovations, constructive and useful inventions and pointedly aggressive against those who would disturb their wives' peace-of-mind.

Few of these mothers had grateful words for their doctors, but the baby's pediatrician often got a good rating. Some mothers claim to have won "converts"—their physicians—who went on to influence other women to try relactation. The majority of doctors exposed to these mothers, however, having had no previous experience, chose to reject the idea.

Two-thirds of all the medical people in contact with this group felt categorically that breastfeeding without pregnancy was impossible." It is non-physiological," one doctor stated! Those medical persons who took a more tolerant approach still

---

° One mother who was not a respondent in this study, withdrew the supplements too soon and found herself with a dehydrated baby. She was so aware, however, that in two days the situation was remedied.

had a "show me" attitude. A few very interested doctors were extremely committed to helping these mothers and learning more about the process. They are now a great influence on other medical people.

The main source of practical information and supportive help came from other women also involved in some way with breastfeeding. The doulas were almost always connected with the La Leche League, that group of devoted women whose mission is to keep other women breastfeeding.

It was they who played the role of doula—assisting, aiding and supporting this special kind of breastfeeding mother. As mentioned before, the doula *can* be a husband or a physician, even a father, but usually is another female.

The mothers of the "borrowed" babies mentioned earlier were so involved with the adopting mother they often not only provided her with advice and encouragement but shopped for her, baby-sat for her older children, etc.

The best doula was the mother who had done it. The role was often performed via long-distance telephone. Many a call calmed a worried relactator and kept her trying.

"I still have the phone bill on my bureau," said a mother who had failed to breastfeed her natural child but nursed the adopted one 11 months. "It was one of the happiest charges I ever paid."

There's an old adage: "Everybody needs somebody." In the case of nursing mothers, experience tells us that almost everybody *must* have somebody.

Why Do They Finally Wean?

When weaning time arrived, the major difference between the natural and the adopting breastfeeders was that lack of milk was *not* a reason to stop nursing. From the beginning, these mothers realized that the quantity of milk was secondary to the nursing experience. When mothers found they had to increase their supplements rather than decrease them, they were disappointed but not despairing. They continued to give the infant whatever they could produce. The nursings, not the milk, mattered most.

"It is certainly not like nursing a 'natural' child," said the mother of three natural and two adopted ones. "It takes much more time, especially at the start. It involves double feedings, breast and supplement, and other people. It demands a firm will-power to weather the slow buildup of milk and a firmer power of will to deal with the outside world. I weaned in order to go on vacation with my husband. I didn't really want to stop."

Would They Do It Again?

"Not only would I do it again, but I can't wait," wrote one mother who was planning to adopt "more and more and more." Most of the mothers felt this way. They listed several essentials for making it work. Patience, strong motivation and a strong ego were foremost. The general impression they tried to convey was that *breastfeeding an adopted child is not easy*. One has to be *determined, supported* and a little adventuresome to succeed.

Only one mother in this sample was negative. She wrote, "I enjoyed it, but really it was too hard and too time-consuming."

The Value of Nonnutritional Nursing

"All right," say the critics, "so the mother is having her way. What about the baby? Is it as important to him as it is to her?" This opens up the crucial question: Which is more important, the act of nursing or the amount of milk?

One place to look for answers is in studies of tension around the mouth and lips of the newborn, a trait human babies share with all mammals. It is a "necessary" tension, one that causes the infant to suck and so stay alive. Without it, he starves.

Human babies with a normal amount of tension frequently have more sucking needs than can be satisfied with a bottle feeding. Bottles empty too fast to satisfy this infantile impulse.

Where the breastfeeding mother may allow her infant to continue sucking, a bottle-feeding mother must give hers a pacifier or let the baby thumbsuck. This nonnutritional (but psychologically satisfying) nursing creates a more contented infant. This has led many physicians to encourage mothers with a short supply of milk to keep nursing, despite supplements so that the baby may have this extra benefit.

There are other aspects of breastfeeding that we are just beginning to notice, such as the value to the baby of skin contact, of smell, of a yielding responsive warm body which is the object of food gratification. Research on the rhesus monkeys at the University of Wisconsin's Primate Laboratories showed that infant monkeys vastly preferred the contact-comfort of an artificial furry cloth "mother" with no milk over a wire "mother" equipped with a feeding bottle apparatus. These animals would drink their fill on the wire "mother," but they clung to and preferred the cloth "mother" the rest of the time.

Further, contact between the human infant and a mother whose heartbeat can be heard and felt has been shown to have positive nutritional and calming effects on the infant (Salk 1962). All these pluses for the breast-nursed baby are extra dividends.

But what about the frustration of a hungry baby nursing on an empty breast? The answer is that if he is hungry he won't nurse very long. He will drop the nipple and in no uncertain terms make his demands heard. No mother can mistake this signal and the mothers of adopted children are usually watching for it.

Success: A New Definition

Three months was the minimum nursing period for any of the mothers. The average time was nine months, many continuing more than a year. The mothers who fed the longest also tended to have the greatest milk supply.

Which of these mothers can be called the most successful? Was it the one who produced the most milk? Was it the one who nursed for ten months with supplements, or another who *never* used bottles but breastfed only five months?

The answer is that we can't determine success in these terms. Success, in a country where there is an unlimited supply of clean milk that can keep almost every child alive, cannot be judged by the same standards used in a country where infants usually die if the mother can't breastfeed. Here we can afford to qualify success, to permit the whole nutritional question to be secondary, for we know the infant will be fed one way or another.

Thus success at breastfeeding in an affluent Western culture is judged by a period of time considered adequate by the mother. It can but need not include supplementary feeding. It is a voluntary act by the mother terminated at her discretion.

Having defined it as such, we can then consider the questions of increased closeness, intimacy and an endearing relationship between the breastfeeding pair. The testimonials from the mothers of breastfed adopted infants demonstrate the value of enhancing the bond.

"I never did get to go without some supplements but what did I care. That was just a small nuisance compared with such a great joy."

In addition, the breastfeeder offers skin contact to the mother which may be as important to her as it is to her infant.

One such mother reminisced that she treasured the memory of this closeness with her infant even more than she had valued it while it was happening. "The warm feelings I get when I remember holding her make up for a lot of things like missing being pregnant and actually going through the birth experience."

Many of the descriptions of feelings ended with statements like: *"It's the mothering that counts." "It's the warmth that one feels." "It was the closest experience I have ever had." "It really cemented the bond with this little creature that was my daughter." "I was so privileged to have him but to have breastfed also was a miracle."*

Hear Ye!

The news is spreading. Recent changes in attitudes towards adoption encourage the dissemination of this new idea. Parents usually tell their children if they are adopted and often discuss it freely in public. The taboos, shame and stigma formerly used against the child and attached to the adopted adult have dramatically changed. It is now the unique person that responds with amazement or thinks that parents should not admit they have adopted their child or children.

In fact, admission of adoption often has an opposite effect. People nowadays tend to look at those who take other people's offspring into their lives with approval and admiration.

The increase in adoptable babies has also brought changes. Despite the many birth control methods, about 350,000 babies are born to unwed mothers each year, many of whom are black or of interracial unions.

More and more of these "unwanted" children are being adopted by white families. The satisfactions of breastfeeding an adopted interracial child are many.

A Creative Experience

Those who look for variation, invention and discovery will find breastfeeding an adopted child a great opportunity. Think of the creativity and complexity we had in this small sample. There were women of all ages, physical and social backgrounds, and experiences. Each mother had to improvise, each had to find her own way, and so each invented a unique method for herself.

The infants too—half males, half females—were a diverse group. Some weak, others strong. Some rugged, some delicate. Some good suckers, others poor at it. Some with a tough gut, others with tender digestion. Some with allergies and others unaffected by anything. Some intensely preferring their mother's breasts, others indifferent.

The best advice for any woman thinking about breastfeeding an adopted child is GO AHEAD AND TRY. Starting with a well-fed healthy infant, create new styles, new ways of experiencing this unique closeness. In addition to the pleasures of breastfeeding, mothers who breastfeed adopted children today have the satisfaction of knowing they are creating a pathway for other women in similar positions, who are searching for ways to make their mothering more meaningful.°

° Though I may not be able to respond, I welcome suggestions and case histories of your experiences as well as old wives' tales, childhood misconception, etc. Please write The Human Lactation Center, Ltd., 666 Sturges Highway, Westport, Ct. 06880

10

Togetherness in Mammals

A UNIQUE KIND OF "COOPERATION" OCCURS AROUND THE delivery time of many social mammals which has important effects on the group. The birth and presence of an infant reinstates, rearranges and intensifies relationships between the mother and other members of her group. It is significant that all this occurs at a time when mother and newborn are most in need of protection and support.

Apes and monkeys do not stop wandering and foraging right after birth. They carry their young with them and keep right on. However, the presence of the newborn infant attracts other members of the group so that they slow down, allowing the new mother to recuperate and keep up with them. This "cooperation" functions to improve the survival of the recently delivered mother and infant.

The composition of the group, during this perinatal period, differs from species to species. Their effect on the mother-infant pair also varies depending on who is allowed to approach the pair, and what they are permitted to do and when they do it.

The Male Cares

Males are allowed to approach the new mother and her newborn in some animals. The gorilla is a good example, because this species has a haremlike family grouping. The female who has most recently given birth stays closest to the silver-backed dominant male. Her companion "wives" are not permitted near the baby, but the male is tolerant of, even attracted to the infant. The mother permits him free access and he indulges this new group member playfully. In her privileged central position, the mother has greater protection and a better chance in the competition for food.

Gibbons live in "nuclear" family groups which include the male-female pair and their offspring. Female gibbons and their partners pair for life. This closeness fosters *paternal* care. In fact, it is the male who cares for the young, returning the infant to the mother only for breastfeeding.

Wolves live in a larger family grouping made up of an adult male-female pair and juveniles of their previous litter. This group actually *assists* the mother for a period after she delivers. The dominant male and the younger animals hunt together, feed and return to the female, regurgitating food for her. As a result, she can remain in the lair with her young. This has survival advantages for the small pups, who would be easy prey for other animals, as well as for the mother who would be slowed down and endangered by their stumbling pace.

The Female Caretaker

The most frequent and complex type of interaction occurs between other females and the mother-infant pair.

The elk, for example, gives birth apart, but within sight or hearing of the band. After a few days the calf is hidden alone or with other newborn calves to await the return of the grazing dam. Frequently one of the mothers "baby-sits" for the calves while the others forage for food.

A curious pattern occurs in the South American raccoon-like coati. Though females of this species live in close contact all during the year, they separate from each other about eight days before they are about to give birth. This happens almost simultaneously because their reproductive cycle is seasonal, so all females give birth around the same time. Each pregnant mother builds a tree nest, has her litter in it, and descends infrequently to eat. Some forty days later, she and her litter come down and rejoin the other females and their young. Because these animals deliver several babies who cannot be carried, they must "hide" them in separate nests. Contact between the young and other females does not happen until the young can move about on their own. Once this occurs, however, their being together provides protection for them and their young.

Very intense female-mother-newborn interaction takes place in many primate groups. Patas monkeys live in haremlike clusters composed of a male and several adult females, with and without young. When there is a birth, the females as a group become very protective of the newborn. They will bitterly attack and chase away even their own male leader if he attempts to come near the infant. Seemingly, this action protects the helpless and possibly very appetizing-looking infant.

Jane Goodall, the famous ethologist who has studied chimpanzees for years in the dense African forest, estimates that one-fourth of all the various groupings observed by her over the years were "nursery groups" made up only of females with their young (1968). These female chimpanzees are in similar stages of reproduction and can benefit each other by staying together. For instance, their foraging pace may be slower than that of other group members without young, or they may choose a terrain less difficult and less exposed to predators of infant chimpanzees, or they may have different dietary needs from nonlactating animals.

Squirrel monkeys are reported to develop close relationships with females other than their mothers. These females act maternally toward them, and if a mother is removed, her infant transfers filial responsiveness to the female with whom he has this relationship. In captivity, if the female is dominant over the infant's mother, she may steal him away from her, and if the infant is still nursing, he may starve to death. In the wild, the mother might be able to regain her infant and keep him only by running away (Rosenblum 1971).

Change in Hierarchy

Many species have ranking systems, with some animals dominant over others. All this is changed when the newborn appears. A temporary rearrangement of social structure occurs. Phyllis Jay, another ethologist who studied langurs intensively, described this change. Immediately after birth, langur babies attract the attention of other female members, and as many as ten of them may surround and try to groom the mother in order to get near the infant. After a few hours, she permits them to hold the baby and even to pass him from one female to another.

No matter how lowly her former status, the mother now assumes a position of central importance. Animals before whom she formerly cowered now act subserviently toward her. All aggression directed against the mother stops. From the moment the infant is first noticed until he begins to mature and the adults lose interest, attention and activity are focused on this mother-infant pair.

The Way of the Elephant and Dolphin

In African elephants ". . . each family unit, composed of closely related females and their calves, acts as an ideal social milieu into which each calf is born. Protective behaviour is frequently seen between members of the family, which is not unreasonable since by doing this they are increasing the survival chances of near relatives with whom they have many genes in common. (Iain Douglas-Hamilton, personal communications 1972)."

Life magazine reported on the pregnancy, labor, and delivery of an elephant in captivity named Belle. Belle had several sessions of false labor. Each time she trumpeted her discomfort, two female elephants housed in adjacent cages became very excited. Focusing only on the birth, confused zoo personnel got alarmed and removed the two agitated females from the area. As a result, a rare chance to observe their involvement in the birth was lost.

Those who have worked with dolphins in the huge tanks on Bimini Island in the Bahamas describe protective responses in the female dolphin. As labor progresses, other females become agitated and withdraw with the pregnant dolphin from the rest of the group. After delivery, they assist the mother by buoying the newborn and the mother, if necessary, on the surface of the water so both may breathe.

The Social Animal

Why do animals cooperate at all? Why do they live together in the first place? What attracts human beings to each other? Why do they live in groups?

We can get some answers from our animal heritage—without denying the unique part which is our humanity—if we are careful not to credit animals with feeling things they cannot feel or doing things they cannot do and to credit humans with animal behaviors they have long lost.

The early theories about why there were social groupings among animals went all out and as a result contain much anthropomorphism. There were those who argued that animals, which could organize themselves best for the hunt ate better, lived longer, and survived to father more offspring than those who hunted alone. This may be so, but then it does not necessarily follow that that's how groups began!

The current theory that males in groups started it all by cooperating during the hunt is a fine idea, except that it leaves out the evidence that most social mammals do not hunt—they forage for leaves, fruit, grasses, etc. Besides, those mammals that hunt usually do so alone, not in groups. Further, early man was also a forager, a scavenger, at best. Finally, one might guess that this theory was proposed by males, for it leaves all the females hungry, alone—in fact, not even there.

Others have theorized that sexual attraction was the dominant instinct that kept animals together. This idea ignores the evidence that adult males and females usually live apart except for a once-a-year short mating season. It is a very common feature to find groupings composed exclusively of only males or of adult females and their young. In fact, only a fraction of an animal's lifespan is concerned with sexual behavior. Take the gorilla or the chimpanzee. Their sexual activity is limited to only a few short periods *per lifetime*. The infant-bearing adult spends most of her life pregnant, lactating, or in the process of weaning in preparation for the next offspring (Van Lawick-Goodall 1968). Moreover, the sexual period, no matter how short, is often a *disruptive, not a uniting experience*. Animals generally pleasant, even passive toward each other, become aggressive during mating periods.

Thus, we must rule out hunting and sexual activities as *the* main reason for the cohesiveness of groups.

One view of why mammals are social beings holds that they have gotten used to the pattern of close living during the long mother-infant period of early dependency. The circle of tolerance for closeness, it is said, widened outward from the intimacy between mother and infant to the tie between litter mates, and then extended into a system of reciprocal responses with other members of the group. Besides, being together is more interesting than living alone. Primates seek out new experiences and get bored easily.

Another suggestion is that patterns of social living may have evolved because individuals survive best in groups. There are more eyes to see predators and more noses to smell enemies. This kind of security means a better defense against those forces that threatened not only the mother-infant pair but the survival of all members in the group.

What Holds Animals Together?

Besides survival, food and sex, I suggest that something about the young of one's own species interests and excites other members and keeps them involved with each other. The attraction to the newborn is felt by the mother, by other females and males in the group, and is a strong cohesive force.

This magnetic pull of the baby that includes both his mere physical presence and his behavior remains one of the few "innate" responses that seem to be rooted in our animal past. Although interaction between the human mother and her baby and between other members of her group and the baby seem often to be structured by habit and tradition, many responses, especially in the first few days and weeks of the baby's life, seem to have a biological basis. Certain infant behaviors appear to trigger automatic responses in adults. These "care-eliciting" reflexes in the infant stimulate very characteristic "care-taking" reactions in the adult.

The *startle reflex* in the human infant is one such example. The baby appears to be shocked. He throws open his arms during sleep and extends both hands with widespread fingers. This spasm is present for only a short time after birth and then disappears. Studying films of many of these episodes (Blauvelt 1962) shows that each time the infant spasmodically spreads his fingers, any adult present and involved with the baby will spontaneously respond by placing his or her index fingers in the palms of the tiny hands. The infant's immediate response is to clutch the fingers, "hooking" the adult literally and emotionally.

The startle reflex may be quite an important experience for the breastfeeding mother. "Catching" the little outstretched hand attracts and focuses the mother's attention toward the infant. It is one way to keep her interest until the milk appears about two days after birth. In the long evolutionary history of human beings, an infant with a very strong reflex could interest his mother and in this manner add to his potential survival. One who weakly or seldom showed this reflexive action might succumb through indifference and abandonment by the mother.

Men respond to this reflex in exactly the same way. While a father's response may not seem important now, once upon a time the reflex may have been a cardinal link drawing early man to the infant or even displacing aggressive feelings toward him.

Another instinctive response is the mother's "covering" reaction immediately after birth, no matter how warm the room or how hot the climate (Raphael 1966). Automatically, she encloses the baby with her hand, her body, or a cloth. Covering helps to raise the temperature of the newborn infant's skin, which lowers after birth as the birth fluids evaporate from the baby's body.

The cooler the infant, the more likely he is to move and the greater the tendency on the mother's part to cover him. She usually "massages" her baby until his skin temperature is the same as that of her hand. This handling occurs unless the mother has had some drugs or the delivery procedure separates the two.

Some actions which adults take for granted may yet be found to be responses to stimuli from the infant. Patting the chest and buttocks, tweaking the chin, nuzzling, kissing, etc., go on all over the world. Mothers tap their hands even when the baby is only within sight or hearing distance. It is likely that this handtapping is another innate adult response to the looks or sounds of a neonate (C. Bateson, personal communications, 1972). These behaviors may be the human equivalents of the licking and nosing responses in other mammals, which function to stimulate the infant's circulation and breathing.

The "rooting" reflex studied so carefully by Piaget is another care-eliciting behavior related to hunger and touch. The infant automatically turns his head, purses his lips, and "roots" (searches) for the nipple. To this signal the mother responds by offering the breast. No matter how inexperienced, most adults who see these movements automatically, perhaps innately, interpret them correctly as hunger.

Usually, this reflex initiates feeding, but it must be responded to or it will not be continued. If the mother is not near, or if she doesn't react, the reflex *disappears* and the baby must then signal that he is hungry by crying.

Before bottles, this "rooting" may have been an important way for the infant to "entice" his mother to respond. Today, as we have mentioned, such intimate contact is no longer vital to the infant's survival, but we can't dismiss it altogether as not important to him or for the mother. Some mothers may need instant recognition of their infants so that feelings of intimacy can be aroused before curiosity is lost and the relationship between them is changed.

The early infant "smile" is a most appealing reflex. Adults cannot wait to see the first signs of this response (coldly described by cynics as no more than a facial spasm), and their reaction of joy appears to go far beyond simple curiosity.

Researchers doing cross-cultural studies discovered that certain types of *smiles* are universal. They find them even in children who are deaf and blind from birth, showing that the smile is not learned through mimicry. Anticipation of a smile may be one of the factors which encourage females to respond to new babies. Even adult males, when playing with infants, work to elicit a smile.

A baby will smile in response to a visual stimulus. Just two eyes, a nose, and a forehead moving on a stick will do. To bring on a smile, you need only stand directly in front of the infant and tilt your head backward with a fairly quick movement. Your efforts will usually be rewarded with a smile, and other adults will marvel at your rapport.

Aside from reflexes, newborn babies have distinctive body *smells* coming from the soft spot on top of the head and the creases around the neck, arms and legs. These odors attract adults and act as care-eliciting factors, but the parent must hold the infant close to experience them. A smell-sensitive father once remarked, "If they could bottle that smell, someone would make a million dollars."

Some animals must *hear* their newborn infant's sounds immediately after birth or they will not be able to identify his cry for help later on. The Cornell University goats we mentioned in an earlier chapter, who were experimentally separated after birth, could not recognize their own kid's distress cry.

Human mothers recognize different types of crying. Fortunately, they can learn to respond even if they haven't heard the infant cry in the first few days after birth. But the effects of separation (such as we have in our hospitals) may *delay* the *strength* of the mother's emotional attachment by days or weeks. The mother who knows the difference between a fussy cry which asks for some rocking and the cry which says, "I'm starved," will be much calmer in her handling, and much less apprehensive when her baby fusses.

Before hospitals became *the* place for deliveries, the mother and baby were tucked into the same bed at home. The infant received a great deal of stimulation and cuddling. It was an excellent setting for each to learn to respond to the other. The baby's body molded itself in response to the mother's movements, breathing, and rhythm. Both benefited. Recent studies confirm that infants exposed to the recorded sound of heartbeats slept better and gained more weight than those who did not hear the same recording (Salk 1962).

Should babies be put back into bed with their mother? This is easier said than done. In the first place, the idea would disturb some mothers because of the aura of sexuality connected with body contact and with beds. In fact, we have come so far that in hospital delivery rooms in most Western countries the mother is prevented from touching her infant after birth for fear of contaminating the sterile delivery "field."

But it's also not easy to repress the innate maternal reaction. Childbirth films show mothers automatically reaching out for their newly delivered infants, only to have a nurse's or doctor's hand intercept hers, hold her back, or actually snatch the baby from her grasp.

We are more concerned about keeping things sterile than we are in allowing the expression of deep and natural feelings. Why can't the responses to these various reflex mechanisms be seen as "love lessons" for the new mother? Many need them for mother love is by no means automatic. In fact, this strictly human emotion can be entirely absent. *Letting mothers respond to the sights, sounds, smell and touch of their newborns can put some of the deeply natural reactions back and intensify the love relationship between the two.* Let's not forget also that others (especially our doula) could be permitted that same contact which might help intensify the bond between them and the mother-newborn pair. We've already discussed the many advantages to that relationship.

Most of these reflexes are short-lived. They disappear even faster if the opportunity does not exist for the mother or others to respond to them. In complex Western cultures, if they are missed, they remain lost opportunities and nothing more, but in primitive societies the sad alternative is usually death for the infant.

No Time for Extras

In less developed cultures, when mother and infant miss the time they need to cement their relationship, there is no alternative. For instance, among the nomadic Lapps of Siberia, childbirth must be subjugated to the life struggle of the group. They are often so pressed by changing seasons which require frantic movement before a river freezes over or a mountain pass becomes blocked with snow that everything else becomes secondary.

Similarly, the camel nomads of the Northwest frontier in West Pakistan spend much of their lives moving their animals from water hole to water hole. Women pray that their children will be born during those periods when the group is encamped and sedentary and the animals are grazing, not on the move. Otherwise, the mother knows that there is little or no support for her and her child. There is no place for recuperation or time to establish the kind of intimacy which assures survival. The average infant death rate in this area from all causes is one in every two born.

Time-Out for Mother

Care-eliciting behavior from the newborn has a better chance of getting an adult's attention if those crucial first days are organized to allow the mother to experience this interaction. This means the participation of others.

The amount of time and support the pair is given varies from culture to culture. In some cultures the emphasis is on the mother, in some on the child. Some give the pair much time, others very little attention.

One factor which determines how much attention is to be given is the value of the new infant to the group. We must not forget that though most people want and treasure infants, in some cultures they come too frequently for the food supply (*see* illustration) and are a tremendous burden to raise. In other cultures or at different times children are in demand as assets, extra working hands, insurance for the parents or sources of bride wealth and one would expect a greater effort expended to have them survive.

There are many different patterns of supportive help. One is for the pregnant wife to remain with her husband or his family for her confinement. Her treatment while in the care of in-laws (or sometimes co-wives) varies from great attentiveness to outright indifference. Much depends on the personality of the mother and the individuals helping her.

The Muslim pattern, where women marry into their husbands'

families, is a less variable, more structured example. These brides move into the female quarters of their in-laws' homes. Strict tradition is used to keep them there for the rest of their lives. Within these closed walls, their infants are born and breastfeeding begins. In general, it is a very protected environment.

Many groups all over the world practice a cultural form of behavior called the *couvade*, where the husband becomes deeply involved during childbirth. As his wife goes into labor, he acts out this and each successive stage as if it were happening to him, dramatizing the contractions of labor and the experience of delivery. Meanwhile, his wife remains as quiet as possible, pretending that nothing is happening. By reversing roles the parents magically divert the attention of any evil spirits so that nothing will go wrong.

This curious trait may seem contradictory and appear to ignore the mother. But even though she is not coddled directly, the indirect effect of this unique role-switch functions to her benefit. Her delivery is being focused upon by many people despite the fact that the male is making the noises and getting the solicitous attention. The whole drama is directed toward helping her and keeping her infant alive.

"If I Had My Way . . ."

An excellent arrangement of intimate care for the mother occurs in India, where the wife leaves her husband and his family and returns to her natal family for the baby's birth. In the majority of the 250 cultures that I looked into, this was the *vastly preferred pattern*, especially for a woman's first baby. We might assume that within the warmth and familiarity of her childhood home the young expectant mother would find the best place for experiencing her introduction to motherhood.

This pattern is what most women would choose if they could. If they had their way they would predominantly choose their "own people" rather than their in-laws or strangers to be around them at this time. If the cultural practice is that pregnant women do not return to their own homes, they prefer their mother, aunt, or sister to come to them, rather than rely on their husband's relatives to assist them during and after the delivery.

It is an emotional, human situation. When one needs tending, one looks to those most intimately related. For most new mothers around the world, the home in which one was a child is the most supportive place to deliver a baby and establish the life-sustaining breastfeeding routine. (We must remember that there are often no alternatives, that there is no freezer, that food must be gathered and fresh each day, that fires must be kindled and supplied with fuel, that human and food wastes must be carried away frequently and that the word "independence" is equivalent to isolation and isolation in underdeveloped societies leads to death.)

Let's see now who does the mothering of the mother in other places on this globe and let's get an idea of how well that mothering works.

11

Mothering Around the World

WE WESTERNERS HAVE LOST OUR BREASTFEEDING FOLKLORE, SO, we had better quickly catch and record the practical and mystical practices from other cultures before they, too, are drowned in the bottle-feeding world. If we don't capture what's left, we'll have to go back to the very beginning and rediscover everything bit by bit.

Missionaries or male anthropologists, our main reporters on how others live, have been loath to look at—even more to see—a bare-breasted female with a baby attached. Besides, no one told them that milk was one of the most absorbing concerns in the female world or that it was the most crucial factor in a baby's life. As a result, we have very little knowledge about how other peoples view breastfeeding and how they make it work. We can usually find more facts and descriptions concerning circumcision, ear-piercing, ritual baths, or infant haircutting ceremonies than data on this life-giving, time-consuming process of infant feeding.

It is only fair to add that in many cases even when males *are* interested in the affairs of women, they find it difficult, sometimes impossible, to get information. Women are often secretive

about female matters and keep them not only from male anthropologists but from *all* males. And they mean it. An ill-fated anthropologist defied the rules of a primitive society in the Philippines that decreed childbirth as sacred, secret, and reserved for
female eyes only. He hid himself in the rafters of the house to
watch a delivery. When he was seen leaving the house, he was
killed.

Even female anthropologists can find it difficult to secure an
invitation to a birth chamber or to get there on time to catch the
delivery. Margaret Mead, who has spent much of her professional life studying matters concerning mothers and infants, told
me that she witnessed only eight births in her first twenty-five
years of fieldwork.

Breastfeeding, of course, isn't quite so private—in fact,
women in most cultures are quite unselfconscious about feeding
in public view. The problem is in the viewer.

Rites and Symbols

If we look and ask questions, we see that breastfeeding is a
fierce preoccupation of most women. It may surprise the reader,
but one of the reasons for this is that it's not an easy thing even
for primitive women.

Though it is true that mammals have been breastfeeding for
millions of years, natural selection has not bred out all the non-
lactators or those with meager milk supply. There is no guaran-
tee that all women will have sufficient milk, especially for the
firstborn child who often does not survive due to the mother's in-
experience at handling infants, and that lactation has not had a
chance to become established and "automatic."

As with other trouble spots in life, when things are important
and failure possible, the supernatural is called on for help. For
instance, the ten-thousand-year-old Venuses of Willendorf, the
hefty, two-inch stone females from the era of the Neanderthal
man, were long believed to be some sort of fertility symbol. (*see*
illustrations.) Only recently have we recognized that the
coiffures of these buxom "statuettes" remarkably resemble the
nipple and areola of a lactating woman. These figures were probably amulets directly related to success in lactation.

Even rocks have magic. Jordanian women collect the white stones from the Grotto of Milk in Bethlehem as amulets. Legend says some drops of milk from Mary's breast sanctified the area, so they believe these pebbles have special powers to enhance the milk supply.

The Japanese manufacture facsimiles of the breast that women buy and present as offerings in special temples, much as Catholics light candles in church. In Iran women visit special religious shrines where they believe prayers for sufficient milk are likely to be answered.

American Indian practices in the past have included rubbing clay and herbs over the body and breasts of the mother, warming her in a heated pit, feeding her reproductive organs of animals, giving her various medical concoctions, using spells and magic bundles—all to make the milk flow.

In some African societies, if the milk doesn't flow, the mother is thought to have been unfaithful. Not until she confesses her indiscretion can she expect to have her milk "come in."

Unlike women in Western cultures, where information about breastfeeding is forgotten, hidden or ignored, those in most other areas of the world recognize many nuances. They know the difference between colostrum and "true milk," for instance. They distinguish between a new mother's milk and the milk from a woman who has been nursing for two or three years. They know what foods give the baby diarrhea and what must be used to cure it.

There are many contradictions in the world's long list of do's and don't's about breastfeeding. We can learn a great deal from them especially since they focus on the trouble spots and often have successful remedies. Their importance for us is that they make us aware of the relativity of rules that work despite the fact that some *insist* that their way is right and others *know* that it is wrong.

On every continent there are reports of pregnant mothers eating earth. This practice, called *geophagy*, may derive from nutritional needs. Analysis of the content of the earth eaten shows that it is usually full of lime and high in minerals necessary for the pregnant woman. In the seventeenth century, Spanish noblewomen ate so much soil that penalties were imposed by government and religious authorities, who feared these women would commit accidental suicide or incur abortions, both of which were sins.

Many cultures separate the infant from the mother for a variety of reasons. The Bushmen of South Africa, for instance, think it's unhealthy to nurse immediately after delivery. They pass the newborn around to other nursing mothers until the "danger" period is over. There's quite a variety of opinion on when the milk is safe. In some cultures it is almost mandatory that the infant nurse immediately; otherwise the women believe problems in breastfeeding are certain to occur.

The Dards, an Asian tribe, use breastfeeding as a symbolic act to cement ties within the clan. Each infant is fed in turn by every lactating mother. Children fed by the same mother, even in this token manner, are considered brothers and sisters, and as such are expected to aid one another throughout their lives. The Palestinian Arabs credit the milk as establishing the mother's tie to the child she has borne. In these cases, breastfeeding is equivalent to birth or marriage in creating kinship relationships.

The tie of milk extends beyond the infant, beyond keeping him alive. The flow of milk assures a woman her status. Her very position in society depends on whether her magic, her rituals work. With so much at stake, it's no wonder these practices are so elaborate and so important.

A Gift of Food

Well-meaning and helpful friends in Western countries often take food to a new mother as a treat or a convenience. In many cultures, however, food gifts are vital. Though ostensibly brought to the mother in celebration of her matrescence, especially in areas where the level of nutrition is low, these gifts are nutritionally important for her milk supply.

Very often these celebration foods, such as meat, are precious not only because they are full of protein but because they are rarely eaten and highly prized. Nevertheless, some of the foods that mothers are required to receive and eat do not always come up to good nutritional standards. Frequently highly valuable foods such as fish and dairy products are *tabooed*. Sadly, most people follow the same practice they use when infants do not thrive on artificial milk; they dilute it. The diet is not questioned nor can it be changed since most other foods are considered bad or even dangerous. So the mother gets less, not more, food and continues to weaken.

Wherever there is breastfeeding there are food "rules." It doesn't matter whether their source of power is medical, religious or magical; for the most part they work. Each new generation is cautioned. Don't eat turnips, they will give the baby gas (Hungarian belief). For more milk, drink malted milk, eat dove meat and veal. If the milk isn't strong enough, supplement it with camomile tea (German sayings). For a good milk supply, boil anise seed in water and drink it three times a day (Armenian). Don't treat your mother-in-law with contempt or the bull's veins will close and you will not get the blood-meat-fat-milk dish after delivery which you need for the milk supply (African). Since the United States is a melting pot of so many nations, there is a rich supply of these cultural adages to be heard if we would but listen.

At times this folklore agrees with Western medical advice. Sometimes not. For those women who are still enveloped in a rich cultural pattern, these prescriptions are meaningful and right, for they are part of a whole complex of rules and regulations that make this period *different* and the new mother *special.* Most of this extra attention works for her benefit, and it is usually appreciated, even enjoyed.

Sexual Taboos—A Necessary Evil?

Among the many taboos burdening the newly delivered mother, those against sexual intercourse are most common and considered a great hardship, at least on the husband. Restrictions range from a few days in some countries to over two years in others. Some societies are not definite about any specific period of abstinence but encourage a pair to stay sexually apart until "all the baby's teeth are in," or until weaning is completed.

In nonindustrial cultures these customs are essential because breast milk is the only source of infant nutrition, and another pregnancy, another baby, almost surely means death to the previous child. Many peoples are forced to practice infanticide if a new infant is born before the older child is weaned, for there is seldom enough milk for two.

The ritual intercourse which is practiced in a few cultures hours or days after birth usually has religious significance. Since ovulation does not occur for at least several weeks, there is little chance of pregnancy resulting from this experience. In some parts of India, this ritual is performed as a precaution to insure that the womb remains "open" so that someday there can be another pregnancy. In other areas, it is believed that this act helps the mother to heal or it is practiced to release the taboos put upon her during pregnancy.

In the United States, where it is popular to determine bodily processes in multiples of threes, it is not surprising that husbands and wives are usually warned not to resume intercourse until six weeks after childbirth. This abstinence is maintained primarily because of our ideas about uncleanliness, healing, and our taboos about sexual intercourse during menstruation.

Weaning—When Is Enough Enough?

The term "weaning" has many meanings. It can mean the point where other foods are *first* introduced, or the time when the breast is no longer offered, or any place between. "We wean at one year" can mean that weaning begins or ends at one year, or it can mean that it takes as much as a year to accomplish, or it can describe the completion of the process. When I use the term "weaning" in this book, I mean *the process* of changing the infant's diet from mother's milk to baby or adult food and methods of eating.

Most human beings do not reckon events like weaning in segments of years or months. The child is merely allowed to breast-feed for many years, even throughout another pregnancy, occasionally during labor, and at times simultaneously with the newborn. However, fear exists in some groups that nursing at these times will take nutrition and the "spirit-life" from the unborn or newborn, so in these cultures weaning starts the moment a pregnancy is noted. Apparently many different times for end-ing breastfeeding work. So far, no scientifically controlled studies exist that indicate one way is better than another.

Extensive research has uncovered a variety of reasons for weaning. Some mothers say they are bored or fear ridicule. Some find the child cranky, which gives them cause and helps them to end the nursing. Prolonged nursing will weaken his body and spirit, say some women in some cultures. Western mothers claim they wean to regain their figures, to prevent spoiling the baby, or to get out of the house because of social pressures. Sometimes they wean to a bottle so that the father can get to know the child better by sharing the feedings—or so it is said.

Weaning is not easy, pleasant, or desirable for all mothers. Often women are not ready to stop and find themselves being bullied into it by others. Their critics say the mother is selfish. They demand that she stop so that new babies can be conceived and added to their group. Reports from the Ngoni of Southeast Africa tell of women running away from their villages to avoid having to stop breastfeeding. Many years ago, a Chinese peasant remarked how sad she was when told by her mother-in-law it was time to start weaning. The only time she had been permitted to sit and relax was when she was nursing her baby.

Many women do not feel deprived by the prohibitions against intercourse while breastfeeding. Others may feel it a privation but refrain nonetheless for they value the intimate experience of nursing their present baby, fear a new pregnancy which would bring it to an end and dread the dangers to the child of malnutrition and other diseases that go along with weaning. When women have such feelings, they may be ambivalent when they do wean. The child, in response to the mother's unconscious and contradictory cues, may find the experience difficult. He may get the message that loss of breast means loss of mother too. His anguished clinging could work against him by being so annoying to the mother that it actually gives her the extra "push" she needs to break this intense tie.

When the child finds it excessively hard to give up his place at his mother's breast, in many cultures, women anoint their breasts with bitter herbs, nicotine, mud, etc. Sometimes a group will feel that only separation will work, so the child is sent to the grand-parents.

In Western cultures a bottle-feeding woman who becomes pregnant does not have to wean. There's no shortage of bottled milk. Yet this child, too, is automatically weaned at a specially designated month or year as is the nurseling.

What determines when this should happen? As we discovered some chapters back, the time of matrescence is less a physical choice than a cultural one. Factors such as an era of permissive-ness or a period of rigidity, even the mother's economic position influence the decision. So it is with weaning.

Often the time decided on, especially in Western societies, co-incides with an attitude about when a baby is no longer a baby. At that time, not earlier, and usually without any physiological reasons, a child begins to look unattractive to adults sucking at the breast or chewing on a bottle. Social pressure encourages the mother to wean, and the infant to "grow up." A two-year-old is a baby in some areas but a "little man" in others.

Most of the world's women are in some state of lactation for their entire reproductive lives and, on occasion, even after men-opause. They nurse one infant until the next one comes along and replaces him. Weaning to them is a natural process that comes about gradually, without fanfare, as both parties become less interested. As with most child-rearing practices, the more experienced the mother, the easier the transition from any stage to the next.

Nonnutritional Sucking

Nonnutritional nursing, that is, nursing when there is no longer milk in the breasts, is not uncommon or repugnant in most societies. As a result, nursing is not limited just to small children. Upset older youngsters are often comforted by the nearest woman who offers her breast for succor. This is confus-ing—even repellent—to Westerners, who view the breast as a sexual object.

Reporting on a community of Indonesians who immigrated to Surinam, South America, an anthropologist described a scene where an adult married woman, concerned over her husband's absence and infidelity, was comforted by sucking at her own mother's breast.

In Bali, Margaret Mead filmed the only sequence we have of a man suckling a baby. In the absence of the mother, he gave an infant his breast to quiet her.

Along the Amazon river women of several tribes raise dogs, pigs, and monkeys for food and gifts. It may be shocking to us but it is not unusual for them to nurse the young of these animals along with their own infants.

Nursing is so natural in most cultures that little girls put their dolls or their pets to their own undeveloped breasts when they play house, unlike our youngsters who imitate what they see and give bottles.

Rebuilding a Breastfeeding Tradition

It should give mothers comfort when things are not going right to know that problems in breastfeeding have been solved by women in every culture and for thousands of generations. Knowing what others do to enhance the milk supply gives us a greater appreciation of the breadth of attitudes about breast-feeding and the enormous variety of methods available for making it work. To know that babies survive all over the world in far less comfortable environments than ours should give us the courage to pick and choose some of those ideas that are appropriate for our needs.

Finally, a deeper understanding of the maternal ways of other peoples gives our own matrescence more depth. It might even make it enjoyable for many of those women who are creative mothers of older children but feel it a chore to endure "that diaper phase." Mothers need all kinds of help, but in some ways our American mothers need the most support. Although once a year on Mothers' Day they are well applauded, there are 364 other days when being a mother is not the most honored role in this society.

12

Mothering the Mother

The Secret of Success

The common denominator for success in breastfeeding is the assurance of some degree of help from some specific person for a definite period of time after childbirth.

I call this help "mothering the mother." Sometimes it takes the form of rituals and prohibitions. Sometimes it means doing chores like housekeeping or minding the baby so the mother can nap, but ultimately it permits the mother time to feel secure and to establish the essential rhythm of breastfeeding.

In non-Western societies where this caretaking is prescribed, if the flow of the mother's milk is disrupted temporarily, several lactating women are usually around to keep the baby fed. Other experienced women are there to calm her, "Be patient, all is well." Reassured by their experience and presence, she relaxes and usually, in due course, adequately nurses her infant. The supportiveness of others has allowed her time to get the ejection reflex established.

Once this rhythm of sucking and letting-down the milk is set in the first crucial weeks, fatigue and tension are less likely to disturb or prevent it. It also follows that the longer the mother is mothered by others, the more secure she becomes and the less prone she is to trouble with her milk supply.

Many people think that the milk will just turn on. They expect that with a bit of good will, the maternal instinct will take care of everything. We've discussed milk failure and shown that a major problem can be the establishment of the ejection reflex. And even maternal instincts often seem unable to withstand the social pressures of a world hostile to breastfeeding, nor can they pull the mother from the occasional doldrums brought on by this new and awesome event of childbirth when it must be experienced all alone.

What is needed if a woman wants to breastfeed is someone, almost anyone, with a helping hand and a willing friendliness to make it possible.

An Experiment in Mothering

How much human contact and reassurance is really required? Is it the same for all women? What does it mean and what does it entail to be well-mothered? I played the doula role myself for many mothers in order to find answers to these questions. I wanted to discover the actual amount of time necessary and the depth of information required to get a nursing mother-infant pair organized.

The mothers I helped were mostly middle-class Americans. The few exceptions were foreign women who spoke English moderately well. They were a particularly important addition to the study, not because they were different but because they reacted in the same way as the American women, though they had grown up in a different culture. All these mothers had been referred to me by a physician or by a concerned friend.

Each of the women I worked with had already begun that cycle of anxiety which leads to lactation failure. Though they were not aware of my study, none of them were treated as objects of research. They knew me as an informed professional colleague or as a friend of a friend who was offering help. I couldn't have had a more ideal arrangement. I was studying a process by living it. I was helping these women to do what they wanted to do and at the same time finding out what it took to be a doula.

All of the mothers were at their wits' end. Though highly motivated to breastfeed, they appeared to be failing to supply sufficient milk. They were discouraged, dejected and no longer able to cope with their screaming infants. Their desperation had prompted their pediatricians to advise the exclusive use of the bottle. Many of them had already started the new routine.

Each baby was between six and ten days old when I visited the mother in her home. My behavior was casual but my purpose unquestionable. I was determined to get that mother nursing again.

Once convinced that she *really* wanted to breastfeed, I dramatically threw out all the nursing bottles. Next, I got her something to drink. Tea, coffee, soda, water, fruit juice, beer—it didn't matter. Whatever she preferred would do. Hardly anyone asked for milk, yet many had forced themselves to drink quarts of it under the impression that "milk makes milk." It may well be that a sympathetic response to milk is important to the mother who believes in this relationship, if only that it puts her more at ease.

The simple act of preparing something to drink for someone was in itself a form of mothering. It was immediately and remarkably effective in reducing anxiety. Many of these women were so upset and had lost so much self-confidence that they asked me to supervise such simple procedures as diapering the baby.

I sat and chatted for an hour or more with each one. During this time the mother relaxed, probably for the first time in days. Almost magically, the infant responded to her calm and fell asleep. We don't know what cues inform the baby that mother is more relaxed, that all is well, so that he goes to sleep. It may be the sound of her voice or the pattern of her breathing or the impression of her movements, but even when an infant is in a room next to the mother he seems to sense her state and respond to it.

As one might guess, when the baby awoke and started feeding, the milk let-down quite abundantly. The baby emptied both breasts and returned to sleep without the usual screaming from hunger and frustration which had sent the mother into such panic. The infant's contentment assured her that she was now releasing plenty of milk. We both felt joy.

At first I made a second trip to some of the mothers. I soon learned, though, that this wasn't necessary. One visit and two or three phone calls to me and one or at most two from me (just to remind them that I was honestly concerned) were all that was necessary to keep these women nursing well.

The telephone has become such an ordinary, necessary and personal part of our lives that we take its impact on us for granted. No matter how many miles away we are, we feel close. We hear the person on the other end as if he were in the same room. It is no wonder it was as effective a means of communicating as another personal visit.

Pediatricians often have an early "phone hour" when mothers may call in questions. One estimate has it that almost one-half of some physicians' practice is conducted by phone. American business gets and gives billions of dollars of advice and orders by telephone. Many supportive groups which work at keeping their members from gambling, consuming excessive alcohol, or even committing suicide, use the telephone as a crucial part of their program. It is not surprising that it works with breastfeeding too.

Most of the questions phoned in to me after the initial visit surprisingly had to do with problems other than breastfeeding, such as fever, bowel movements, vaccination reactions, and so on. Most of them could be answered by any woman or man who had cared for young children. In fact, many mothers knew the answers. What they were really calling for was confirmation, reassurance and support. And I was there to give it. That was the whole secret. I was available, interested and happy to help.

The joy of this kind of success runs deep and remains as a lovely memory for a long time. I was reminded of this one day by a long-distance phone call I received from a woman in Wisconsin. Her name was familiar, but for a moment I could not place her.

"Doctor R.," she said, "you may not remember me, but I'm the woman you helped when I was trying to breastfeed and I was so desperate. Well, it's Eric's second birthday today and I just had to call and thank you."

13

The Doula—How It Works
and How to Make It Work

WOMEN NEED SUPPORT IN ORDER TO LACTATE. IN FACT, AS I'VE
just shown, if they get such help even failures can be reversed. I
doubt that breastfeeding can proceed in our bottle-feeding culture without a doula. It would be the rare woman indeed who
could manage such a feat, particularly with her first child. So our
next step is to discover who these doulas are, where to find them,
and how to use but not abuse them in that vital process of helping the mother and the infant get organized.

Who is the Doula?

In one part of the world a co-wife is the doula, in another it's
the mother-in-law. In still a third culture, it's the friend who
went through the puberty rite ceremonies with the now pregnant woman she will help. In America, there is no special person.
The pregnant woman has to go out and find herself a doula.

Planned Doula-hood: The Grandmother

The most ideal set-up is a loving daughter-mother pair—two
people who have lived close to each other and are additions to

each other's lives. Less ideal relationships also work if both parties approach the planning of this period honestly and realize it will only be for a short time. Even when personalities make the relationship less than perfect, the grandmother (either one) as doula is often the most expedient and, in the long run, a saving grace. The Gordons, whom we mentioned in an earlier chapter, show that the presence of a supportive woman often staves off postpartum depressions.

If the relationship leaves something to be desired, don't be hasty and throw out the idea altogether. Mother's mother can still be helpful and appreciated if both parties want it enough to take into account the pitfalls I consider in the Guide presented further on. The relationship must be carefully arranged and limited, and both must agree that the mother's peace-of-mind and her breastfeeding are ultimately the best possible solution *for the baby.*

This period may be one of mixed joy for the grandmother for it confirms to her that her own reproductive life is over and that she will never again cuddle an infant of her own. No matter how much she may be enjoying her new freedom, the presence of a grandchild whom she is yet to know and love, tells her she's no longer young. It's different in India or Japan where this older stage is the most desirable time of life for a woman. Finally she's free to be herself! After so many years of being subordinate, she is now given a daughter-in-law to "boss"!

Getting older in our youth-oriented society actually means losing stature. By being sensitive to the feelings and plight of the new grandmother, the new mother can help make this postpartum period a joy for all, with the miracle and excitement of the baby as the focal point. By forgetting that grandmother has feelings too, one can create a nightmare of usurped privileges and deep resentments resulting in milk failure for the new mother and depression for both.

Who Else Makes a Good Doula?

Our families are so small we have very few alternatives. Having a sister in Alaska while the new mother is in Texas is not much help. A brother's wife, though, who is favorable to breast-feeding and is nearby may be a great choice.

There is an interesting and often neglected group of women whom the anthropologist, Ray Birdwhistell, identifies as the non-gendered females. These are married and unmarried women, female in every way except that they cannot or will not reproduce. Their social positions vary from culture to culture, from the supremely honored vestal virgins in Rome to the low status, ridiculed old maid of Western society.

Until recently, in many places only women who bore children and added desired members to the group were honored. Now with our over-population motherhood is no longer such a superior state, and these nonreproducing women are coming into their own. Not only are they needed by society in business and in the professions but their status as caretakers of children in the roles of substitute mother, teacher, nurse, etc. is rising. The time is right for them to assume the role of doula for the woman who does give birth. Both could be equally interested in the child's welfare and equivalent in status within their group.

Reciprocal Doulas

Some mothers do not have relatives or close friends near them, or they find it impossible to seek their help. These women should consider the *reciprocal* doula.

In this situation two women in similar stages of reproduction become each other's doula. They ought to live near each other and be scheduled to deliver several months apart. The two women may be friends, but friend*liness* and not friend*ship* is the real quality needed. An obstetrician's office or a hospital clinic is an excellent place for meeting possible candidates. We discuss other meeting centers later on.

Many women in this country grow up never having taken care of young children and certainly never having handled a newborn. If such a neophyte could play a reciprocal doula to someone who will have her baby first, she could gain invaluable experience by working with the new infant, while at the same time she is helping the new mother. Even without the doula relationship, she might seek out a brand new infant whom she could bathe, handle, and nuzzle and, in the process, learn how to care for a neonate.

Some women need a minimum of mothering. Sometimes only two hours each afternoon is sufficient to make them feel rested, refreshed, and secure. Just knowing that someone is there in an emergency is enough for them. Others need a great deal of time and physical help to get them organized in their new role. In these cases, the partner must be chosen for her ability to give that required amount of mothering.

Quite naturally, two women making arrangements to become each other's doula will find they have different needs, and some of these will become apparent only after the birth takes place. Nevertheless, first priority and major efforts must be directed toward the requirements of the newly delivered mother, especially in the first few weeks. True, physical needs and daily chores are important, but beyond this, *supportive interaction is the most precious mothering each can offer the other.*

The people who are skeptical about the ability of women to make contact with each other in such short order forget the central focus, the infant. They don't realize the attraction of this little creature and the sudden and sustained excitement that follows childbirth. They haven't experienced the goodwill and *desire* to *give* which women feel toward each other during this period—especially breastfeeding women. It not only can, but it does work.

Do-for-yourself Mothers

A few women have successfully programmed self-study breastfeeding into their lives instead of using other people. These unique women claim they were on their own and alone during the first few weeks after birth, that they used their own intuition and knowledge, and that they breastfed by their own initiative and willpower. There is one thing they did not think to mention. Only intensive questioning revealed that during their pregnancy they learned as much as possible about lactation from technical manuals, popular articles, and any other available printed sources. When they had problems concerning pregnancy, delivery, and child-rearing, as well as breastfeeding, their response was to reach for a book. They followed the advice they found. To them, books acted quite effectively as doulas. Of course, these women are rare. Most mothers need other people and prefer them no matter how inadequate or mediocre their help.

It is exciting however to know that other ways also work—an indication that use of such media as radio or TV might be very effective in keeping some women breastfeeding when personal doulas are not available to them.

The Father as Doula

There is much talk these days about the males sharing the responsibility of child-rearing even from infancy. Here's one area where a man can do his share by playing the doula role for his breastfeeding wife.

The baby's father is an excellent doula if he is available (often not the case) and if he is aware of what is needed. He must also realize his own needs in this new patrescent stage and be able to manage any negative feelings so they do not interfere with his wife's peace of mind.

Two of the most successful doulas I ever came across were new grandfathers. One was a doctor. The other one, who had just retired, was deeply concerned about his daughter and was both amusing and creative in the handling of his new granddaughter.

What it comes down to is this: playing the doula is one of those few experiences in life when answering someone's deep need can offer the giver an equal reward.

Let's look now at what has to be done to make sure that it works.

Guide to a Supportive Relationship

It is one thing to choose a doula; it is quite another to live with one. No matter who it is, the doula's presence and function is new within the life pattern of most Western women. Since no precedent exists in our cultures for the behavior of either the mother or her doula, ways to permit this relationship to work have to be invented. We must organize two people to participate in and enjoy an intense experience of short duration.

I suggest that mothers use what I have called the Interaction Guide for the doula-mother pair. This is a program designed to help bring two individuals into a relationship where the ultimate goal is the contentment of the new mother and the success of her breastfeeding.

Each of the suggestions should be discussed point by point by the pair. If they wish, it might be done in the presence of husbands, older children, in-laws—whoever will be involved or even present during the postnatal period. Sometimes a one-to-one discussion gives each person more room to express deep feelings. If this is the case, the third party should be invited in on the discussion later on.

Whatever is decided should be *written down!* Minutes, days, hours, as many as possible, are best recorded before the decision is forgotten. This may save a great deal of tension later on.

Specifying each role—when, how and for how long—can actually save a relationship and a mother's milk supply. Such a list, taped to a conspicuous door or wall and checked frequently, is the best insurance against misunderstanding.

In going over this Guide together, the partners should decide if it is the activity of the doula that is to be reciprocated or the amount of time that is involved. Since the new mother and the doula will not always do equivalent chores for each other, it is wise to keep in mind that it is more pleasant to do the job you like best. The aim of the discussions is to organize work and relationships into a mutually rewarding experience.

If time is to be the commodity of exchange, one hour given for each hour received is a good starting point for some. Not everyone is satisfied by this kind of arrangement. For some, one hour of ironing is worth two hours of baby-tending or five hours of "sitting" for an older child.

While it is not easy to be free and to allow oneself to say what is deepest in one's mind, nevertheless, honesty during the initial discussions is a most valuable quality. This is often what decides the outcome of any interpersonal arrangement, and the following Guide should be used as extensively as possible to offset personal shyness. Use of the Guide has helped many a mother-doula partnership become a creative adventure.

AN INTERACTION GUIDE TO THE DOULA-MOTHER RELATIONSHIP

The Activities

If the doula comes to live with the mother—both parties should decide in advance who is best at doing which job. If the doula prefers to do chores around the house, she might be happiest doing just this, leaving the mother free to care solely for her new infant. Or they can alternate.

If the doula commutes to the mother's home—other kinds of work arrangements need to be discussed. But the division of labor still must be decided. Perhaps the doula might cook at her home and bring meals to the new parents as her contribution. Perhaps she might take an older child to a daily sports activity or to a weekly lesson, thereby lessening the emotional and physical pressure on the new mother.

If the doula is an older relative—here is yet another area for creative reciprocation. In this instance, there is no possibility of creating a reciprocal exchange of services as can two women in the same reproductive stage. So in exchange for her services, the doula might enjoy an occasional movie with the new mother while the father baby-sits. Or, perhaps, if the doula doesn't drive, an excellent way to compensate her for her kindness would be to chauffeur her on shopping trips, to visit a friend, to keep some appointments—either while the baby sleeps in the backseat, if the mother drives, or while mother and baby stay at home and father does the driving.

As for the mother—she too must frankly state the jobs she likes best, the ones that tire her most and the work she finds a real chore. She particularly must admit those aspects of house or baby that make her uncomfortable. For instance, many women fear that their maternal prerogative is violated if they cannot care for their infants completely. Other mothers must do the household shopping in order to feel in control of their own lives. Some even feel this way about cooking—it is this particular work which makes them feel like wives.

How to say thank you is difficult for many. Some mothers have settled it by baby-sitting for their companion's children for a weekend or a two-week vacation once they have gotten on their feet. One woman gave her doula a valuable Burmese kitten after she had helped her through the first two months with her infant. There are innumerable ways, but money is not usually the best means. The essence of the relationship is reciprocation, a two-way giving, not a payment for services.

As for the husband—if he is the doula—his activities and position should also be carefully planned so that he too won't feel swamped with the sudden pile up of new things to be done. He might prefer to care for the newborn a set number of hours each day (like two hours after dinner) leaving an older youngster with his mother.

Matters Of Time and Place

The doula must frankly tabulate how many hours each day she can give the new mother and how many she must keep for herself and her family. She will have to determine and plan this in advance. She must decide where she can best spend her time in behalf of the mother, possibly at her own home minding the newborn, if she lives nearby. Sometimes weekdays are best because the new father can often stay home and take over the supportive doula role on weekends.

The reciprocal doula who is pregnant is in a unique position. She may be free to baby-sit for the mother's older children or work with her companion's new infant, storing up hours to be reciprocated later on when she delivers.

The mother may need to get away, even if it is only into her bedroom for a few hours alone each day, and may find this the most helpful thing a doula can do for her. She may be a morning person or she may be more efficient with her youngster in the afternoon. She may need a consecutive stretch of hours in one day, three times a week, or a little bit of time every day; but she had better discuss this in advance if she wants her introduction into matrescence to be a joyful experience.

Fathers must speak up too. Some will need peace and quiet after work and others may want to be alone with their wives when they get home. Still another sort may want the mother and the baby to themselves at that time. Speak up, and in advance!

How Long Is Long Enough?

Enter the doula—when? Exit the doula—when? As much as possible determine in advance how many weeks or months the doula is available and how many of those weeks or months the mother may need her help.

The grandmother doula, too, might be more at ease if she knew approximately when the cut-off point would occur, when she would be free to return to her home to resume her normal routine.

The mother might be more comfortable if she could estimate an approximate final date when her home and her baby would again be hers. The opposite might be true of a mother who would only feel easy knowing she had "extra time" owed her and was therefore free to call upon her doula even after the first critical weeks were over and she was firmly set in her breastfeeding.

Some fathers welcome additional relationships; others hate them. Each type should have a say in the matter so that adjustment can be made and compromises settled for the ultimate comfort of the mother and baby.

Things Personal and Particular

Many doulas have special preferences and needs. In the past I knew a woman who had to have a radio playing if she were to cook. Another hated rock music in the morning and the sound of vibrating machines. Special diets were a real chore to a third new mother, but she still appreciated how her doula needed special food to make her feel at home. She found it pleasant to accommodate her. One doula who enjoyed eating meat found herself in a house full of vegetarians. Another loved doing for the new mother but refused to do any entertaining of visitors. She thought they should stay home and said so in no uncertain terms. And then there's the whole thing about animals—some people love them and others are afraid even of kittens.

The grandmother-doula may be very ambivalent about this interrelationship. She may feel the need of being wanted; she may adore the idea of being with her new grandchild; but she may equally fear being exploited. She may be anxious about being used and discarded and hold back such great and loving help because she also is afraid to discuss these matters. *Talk* is the way to free the doula-grandmother to give help and receive love without being hurt.

The mother too has her fears. She may love the doula-grandmother but also fear her. She might worry about being "taken over." She too must look inward, hopefully, even before she delivers, to discover and then communicate her most pressing concerns. She would be wise to face a possibility that some parts of her matrescence may be difficult and that at times she may need to ask for emotional support from her doula. A new mother lonely and far from her own home and friends may need a bit of mothering once her infant arrives.

"Not me," say some women. For these mothers, the very last thing they want may be mothering. They may be eager to have help on matters of breastfeeding and that's that, nothing more.

Visitors in other cultures, who come to congratulate a new mother and greet the new group member are often wined and dined and entertained by everyone *but* the mother. In the

United States, however, there is usually no one else to entertain visitors and this can really create a problem if they are important to the new mother. Here's one area where the doula can help. She can do the entertaining when the mother is tired, or take the infant for a walk if the mother wants to visit with her friends alone.

New mothers early in the postpartum period often feel very pressured because the change in activity has perhaps never been so drastic. Even simple jobs like sending out birth announcements or getting her hair washed, which used to be so simple, to say nothing of painting the baby's room, now never seem to get done. A mother must not be shy to ask her doula to give her time for what she fears may be looked upon as trivial. Helping out in these matters may make all the difference between a mother feeling relaxed or out of control.

Occasionally husbands feel displaced by their own new infants. Channeling energy into a creative doula role or into helping another person play doula for their wives may be a great help. Participation often eliminates the impression of being separated. Husband's needs are no different from the mother's. It's just that when it comes to child-rearing we tend to exaggerate or joke about male participation. The new father may be glad to play doula during the week but needs many work hours for his projects during the weekend. He may want to do the cooking but not the dishes. He may enjoy holding, rocking or walking the baby but despise diaper-changing. He may want to carry on a conversation at dinner but have breakfast without a word. He may want company when he bowls but require absolute privacy during his early morning warm-up exercises. A man plays doula very well if he's given the same consideration, the same chance to choose or reject chores as any other doula.

Talk, talk and talk about these problems to keep them insignificant or even eliminate them. Little things mistakenly ignored build up very quickly. If mutual admission of foibles is permitted from the beginning of the mother-doula relationship, the first few weeks of the infant's life will be a pleasurable experience and not a struggle.

On Space and Privacy

Americans, on the whole, prefer a lot of space around them. Instead of sitting near the stranger in a half-empty theatre, they deliberately choose space farthest away. The same thing happens on an almost empty beach. So, in arranging even a temporary visit, it is most important to keep this in mind if living together, as suggested, is to work.

When the doula lives with the parents, a real attempt to make her comfortable is the beginning of a relationship that says, "I care." There are some simple things which make big differences such as arranging the most satisfying place to sleep, providing a place where she can be alone occasionally, making arrangements for tending the infant without having to lift too high or bend too low, and so forth.

Some mothers prefer to breastfeed their infants in private not only away from guests—even relatives—but away from the doula as well. Even the presence and interaction of an older child can be a disruption. Small things? Yes, but important.

Fathers, too, need time alone with their new infants. They may want to show affection in a very private and personal way. Everyone should see that each person has time with the infant alone.

Almost every household has special places preferred by its inhabitants. A husband may have his den, a wife her bedroom, a doula a quiet corner especially for morning coffee.

Almost all persons in a household have special times when they need to be alone. A prearranged signal which says to all participants, "I would like to be left alone" and another that is a sign indicating "I am uncomfortable about something, let's talk," is a useful way to keep a breastfeeding mother very happy and the baby well filled.

A Sum-up

These are only suggestions intended to stimulate discussion. Each doula-doula couple, each husband-wife team, each doula-mother pair will find their own balance, their own patterns, their own way of giving. There is so much variety in human relationships, I want to caution the reader a bit more. Be prepared for (but don't be alarmed about) the mother who is more comfortable with an arangement that demands her time but makes no personal demands. She may be the kind of person who does not want a friendship relationship but only a working reciprocal plan. The same goes for the doula who will play her role in an equally businesslike fashion, who wants to be effective and rewarding but shies away from the usual chatting and personal interaction many doula-mother relationships include.

Be on the alert for those who are more comfortable with *giving* than with *getting back*. They too make wonderful doulas for the new mother if she in turn is appreciative and unselfconscious about receiving and not compulsive about giving back each thoughtful act.

Wise is the mother who is sensitive to a husband who is a very private person, who will give of his time effectively but take no delight in socializing. A husband's undercurrent of anger can directly affect the new mother's milk supply.

New mothers and fathers naturally tend to be so caught up in the excitement and responsibility of this new package of demands and noise and love that they often forget that not all others are equally concerned. A step back and a pause will give a parent a more tolerant view of why others are not always as involved with their offspring as they are.

Some Do's and Don'ts

Don't take advantage of each other even when the opportunity presents itself. The young mother must be especially careful of the older doula, who is often made to feel exploited in so many areas of her life.

Don't be afraid to ask for help. Don't keep convincing yourself, new mother, that you can do it alone. We do each other great harm by not asking. Asking gives the giver the freedom to make a similar plea for help. In the case of the mother-daughter arrangement a mother who never "imposes" on her daughter is saying, "You can't do it to me either." Another mother who says, "I need you," frees her daughter to say the same. It allows her to say, "Now, I need *you*. Come."

Do not assume, no matter what your age, that *your* way is the *only* way or even the right way. No two people have exactly the same idea about how babies should be brought up. Even sisters raised by the same mother have different approaches.

Don't give advice unless asked, and even then make sure the questioner is really asking for an answer. Older people often feel they are not filling their role unless they give advice. In some instances it is most valuable, but it often runs contrary to the ways and methods of others. It is wise to keep in mind that differences in ways of handling newborn infants are usually choices between two fairly equal methods and almost never a choice of life-or-death proportions. Whatever the mother is most comfortable with is generally the best for the baby. A good point to remember is that a study of babies brought up on a strict scheduling of food and those who were allowed to determine the spacing and amount of their feedings demonstrated that as adults they were equally brilliant and happy people. The important variables were parental self-assurance and real, giving, love.

Another "don't" concerns hiding anguish or anger. If you feel your doula or mother-companion is not pulling his or her weight, or is doing more than you can manage to repay, or has forgotten that you really don't want too much conversation or personal relatedness, *then say so!*

Finally, we must not forget that the relationship must end. If a new friendship develops out of the time spent doing for each other, all the better. But it should not be the main purpose. The reason for establishing this supportive network is to get mothering for the mother. If I were to choose one factor which I thought would best make this partnership work, I would say it was the full realization of the contribution the doula was making. By helping a mother with her introduction into motherhood, by permitting her to feed in her chosen way, the doula is starting a lifetime relationship on a positive note.

14

Help from the Outside—
Present and Future

SOME DOULAS MAY KNOW ABSOLUTELY NOTHING ABOUT breastfeeding. Yet they have a magic way of creating a relaxed circle around the mother. They can project an air of security and supportiveness within which the mother feels free. They make it easy for her to give herself without fear to the relationship and the job of feeding. That's all some mothers need.

If the doula is knowledgeable about breastfeeding, so much the better. If not, the mother need not worry for she can enjoy her doula and turn to the "experts" in the La Leche League with her breastfeeding questions.

Where to Get Breastfeeding Know-How

La Leche League International (L.L.L.I.) was formed by a group of nursing mothers for the sole purpose of supplying other nursing mothers with breastfeeding information. There are thousands of local chapters all over the country. The central office°
will put any questioner immediately in touch with someone at the branch nearest her home.

° La Leche League International, 9616 Minneapolis Ave., Franklin Park, Illinois
60131. Counselling phones: 312-455-7730.

Local groups are led by women who have been trained by the League and who are or have been nursing mothers. They hold home discussion meetings to familiarize women with the many aspects of breastfeeding.

The League members also frequently exchange ideas in other areas of child-rearing. At the same time a mother with a sore nipple is learning about an alternate position for holding her baby, she may also be told about a new diaper pin or an exercise to tone up flabby muscles.

La Leche League members are really "pros" in the art of breastfeeding and thoroughly conversant with almost any breastfeeding situation which may arise. They are particularly adept at reversing the pattern of failure we described in chapter 12, where the mother of an eight- or ten-day-old infant is thrown into panic and depression and already has a supply of bottled formulas in the refrigerator. Rarely can one find a physician who is as well-informed on the procedures and the common problems of lactation—not to mention the emotional needs of the mother.

L.L.L.I. itself functions as a doula-at-large since its members offer help at most any time. A new mother can seek help from one of the women she meets at a meeting of the local group. Or, if she can't attend any meetings, she can call and be given the name of a mother to contact when she needs her.

An expectant mother can use the group's resources to find another pregnant woman with whom she can establish a reciprocal doula relationship. Even the woman who bottle feeds can use their help to find a doula. After all, breastfeeding is only one part of the whole child-parent experience. Being mothered is also an important contribution to the bottle-feeding mother.

Childbirth Organizations Offer Support

There are other places where a mother can look for help in organizing her postpartum weeks. There are groups whose major philosophy, though often understated, involves *supportiveness*.

One of the oldest is the Grantly Dick Read "school" of natural childbirth. This method of delivering a baby (originally developed in England) offers pretraining for the mother and constant support from the doctor or midwife. Clinics for expectant parents, often attached to university teaching hospitals, offer instruction in everything from how to deliver the baby yourself in an emergency, to the latest salve for diaper rash.

Centers where pregnant women gather, such as maternity clinics, would appear to be natural places to initiate breastfeeding programs for the new mothers. In practice, the heavy work schedules and the philosophies of many of those presently in charge, rule them out at least for the present. Hopefully, in the near future they may become responsive to new practices of support, childbirth, and breastfeeding. In any case, these places are centers where women can find other women in similar stages of reproduction and talk with them about reciprocal mothering and doula care.

Support Is Built Into ASPO

Another natural childbirth method is called *Accouchement sans Douleur* (childbirth without pain or sadness). The American equivalent is the "Lamaze group" or the ASPO—the American Society for Psychoprophylaxis in Obstetrics, Inc. Besides the doctor, a *monitrice* (an accredited teacher-nurse) guides the prospective mother through her pregnancy. Originally, the monitrice played a supportive role during labor and throughout the delivery, but the pressures of time and shortage of personnel have ended this complete participation. Now the monitrice primarily teaches this method to expectant mothers and their husbands. She is in a prime position to be the instrument through which women get in touch with each other to organize their postpartum care.

The VNA Is a Natural

Other organizations interested in childbirth will ultimately include the doula concept in their programs. One of the most natural groups for this role is the Visiting Nurse Association. Not only do many branches of this organization have programs for educating pregnant women, but they are in a position to get prospective doula-mothers together. Those nurses who are interested in postpartum care could themselves play the doula. The VNA's goals of ministry and support are exactly what new mothers are looking for.

Mother's Helper Agencies—A Friend in Need

Some state and local groups maintain mother's helper agencies to fill in when there is a crisis in the family. A paid homemaker will go to the house, care for children, do light housework, shop, and prepare meals. What one is doing here is paying a stranger to "care." While this service is often an enormous financial burden, it sometimes turns out to be the only way for a mother to gain recuperation time when a delivery has required surgery or to get the mother some "mothering" when she is depressed. Part of the training for these positions could be information about what is required of a doula and how to be one.

Trends of the Future: Maternity Centers for Mothers!

The general discontent with the matter-of-fact medical-way-of-birth in this country and many new and radical changes permeating our culture, offer hope for a change in maternity care. The future will see maternity centers apart from hospitals organized to take care of the emotional and physical needs of pregnant, delivering and lactating women. Childbirth will be handled as if it were a natural event, not an illness. Mothers will be treated as people delivering human infants, not as dependent patients whose babies belong to the nursing staff.

Medical personnel attached to these centers will be there primarily for emergencies, while the main direction of the delivery will be handled by experienced midwives, and the postpartum care by those experienced in breast and bottle-feeding.

Adult females will be given the kind of attention and care during maternity that *they* want. No mother will have to face delivery alone or in fear. Nor will she be subjected to the isolated homecoming or the all too frequent panicky nursing situation.

Women will be encouraged to move to these centers for a period of time before and after delivery. They could have some of their family with them or go to the center only for instruction and support until the infant is born. The function of this pre-de-

livery time will be to literally get comfortable with their motherhood long before they are asked to leave the center and take
care of an infant in isolation at home. This is indeed the only hu-
mane way to begin living with one's offspring—to start a life together that will span decades of what hopefully will include a
growing and maturing love.

The New Trends: Communal Living, Mutual Giving

Young women today who live communally are already delivering their babies and breastfeeding them within a warm supportive atmosphere. The tenderness and reciprocity that is often a
part of this new life-style spills over into the maternal situation.
With everyone playing doula, caring for the new mother and
fussing over the newborn, she breastfeeds without difficulty.

The question now is to find ways of programming protective-
ness and support into the lives of those of us who live in more
traditional patterns. Now that the majority of Americans live in
nuclear families, we are ever aware of our own isolation and of
how nice it is to have others involved with our babies and children in a more than perfunctory way. We are learning, often the
hard way, how vital it is to have others around who care and
who willingly give help when needed. Not that we wish to go
backward and give up our independent family. It's a matter of
how to have one's apartness without losing necessary and intense
human contact.

New Life Styles: The Joining Families

One way to respond to these needs is for two families to join
and live together, thereby extending the nuclear family horizon-
tally. This living pattern is not as full as the three-generational
family of the past, but it does satisfy many of the basic human
needs lacking in our present frayed culture.

Two young couples with their offspring living in adjoining
houses or in the same apartment house is a second variation of
this theme. Next best would be houses close enough so that
going back and forth would be feasible.

There is a great difference between this type of relationship
and that of the usual friendship practiced by couples today, in

that this arrangement involves a deeper commitment. These "families" would pool many resources. The men could divide many chores and their wives save much time by shopping for each other, caring for each other's children, offering mutual doula help when necessary, cooking one meal in lieu of two, and so forth.

Reciprocating time allows both women to use their abilities and prevents them from feeling frustrated, angry and inadequate. Time given for one woman's piano lesson can free another woman for a swim at the "Y" or a third to teach.

Other Solutions

Many people have suggested that day and night care centers for children are an answer for women's need to do more than child care. They propose that we channel millions of dollars and equal numbers of hours into organizing such places. But this is not the answer for the demands on the mother during this early infant adjustment period. One thing we have learned about children in the past few decades is that they do best *in early infancy* if they are principally cared for *by their own mothers*. Given a reasonably stable household and a level of economic stability where the children can receive all the emotional and physical benefits offered to the general population, mothers responding to their own children are still best. The mere mathematics of hours available does not permit the caretakers in day care centers to give each baby the time and response he would receive from a mother even if she were at home only part of the time.

Mind you, I am not suggesting that day care centers for older children aren't useful. I am saying that they are usually not appropriate for this very early stage of motherhood.

One thing is certain. Mothers and children need mothering and lots of it. Programs that permit mothers more time away from their children but leave those offspring feeling lost and uncared for, save no one time and ultimately put enormous financial pressure on society to correct the damage done.

Women must lobby for time off for childbearing for themselves and for their husbands. They must make others realize that time for this purpose cannot be determined as if all people were alike or all mothers needed the same amount of time to get themselves established with their new babies. Enough time for one mother could mean four weeks. That would be sufficient to get her milk supply flowing so that if she were away five hours a day the supply would not be affected. Another mother might require six months before she was willing to leave the baby or before her milk supply would permit it.

Furloughs for Reproduction (F.F.R.) should be built into most professions (including education) and all other jobs. This will not only improve the status of childbearing women, but it will help them to do a better job of it for they would not feel trapped or resentful. They will know that a place is reserved for them when they want to go back to school or to other professional work. They will also find that with this concept of F.F.R. comes the acceptance of a gradual return-to-work arrangement.

The Gift of Mothering

The amount of mothering a woman needs and how much she actually gets are often two different things.

The optimum situation is one where a mother and her married daughter, on loving terms with each other, live in the same house, creating a three-generational pattern with a full complement of age groups and experiences. The minimal amount of mothering that can also keep some women breastfeeding is a familiar, caring voice at the other end of a telephone. The important thing is to recognize the range of possibilities and hope that the many alternatives discussed in this book will allow mothers to realize their different levels of need and arrange to fill them as completely as possible.

Mothering the mother gives the new parent time to cuddle, care for, and love her own infant. It gives her the chance to watch the baby and build a schedule around that infant which is compatible with her own preferences. It allows the mother to enjoy her matrescence and not find it a burden or a nightmare. Help from others allows this to happen.

Although we have focused primarily on the need of the breastfeeding mother, the support which a doula provides is often just as important for the emotional well-being of the woman who is bottle feeding. The difference is that if the breastfeeding mother doesn't get this support, she must endure, in addition to anxiety and fears of inadequacy, the heartbreak of failure and often a disruption in the relationship with her infant, who now becomes the center of her frustration.

Women who have the will to breastfeed are a special breed, happily growing in number. They enjoy having and nursing babies, but many of them find it desirable to limit their reproductive years. Many are aware that they will seek new fields of study and work after these years are behind them. So they conclude that if this childbearing period is to be such a short stage, they are going to live these years intensely.

Breastfeeding can be one of the greatest enrichments of this special brief time. All efforts to make it work are well worth it.

Without question, a mother will succeed if she is well-equipped with a solid background of information, and if she is cherished, pampered, coddled and respected by other adults who sincerely want her to achieve this very personal and tender gift.

GLOSSARY

Ablactation The absence of lactation. Also, the process of weaning and the cessation of milk secretion when suckling stops.

Agalactia The absence of milk secretion after childbirth.

Agalorrhea The arrest of milk flow.

Alveoli Small cells which form the terminal portion of the alveolar gland where milk is secreted and stored. Alveoli are found in other body tissue as well as in the mammary gland.

Androgalactozemia Oozing of milk from the male breast due to irregular glandular function.

Areola The ring of darkened skin around the human nipple.

Beestings (best' ings) First milk of a mammal after parturition; colostrum.

Breastfeeding The secretion of milk from the human female breast, and the sucking of the infant to provide nutrition immediately after birth and for a number of months (years) thereafter.

Buttermilk Fluid that remains after removal of butter by churning.

Butyrometer Device to measure the amount of butterfat in milk.

Caked breasts Stagnation of milk in the secreting ducts. Sometimes called "milk fever" but it is not a true breast infection since in most cases there are no bacteria present. (See also *milk fever* and *galactopyra*)

Caseation The transformation of tissue into a cheesy mass.

Casein A derivative of caseinogen which forms milk curds.

Caseinogen The principal protein in milk from which casein is derived. Sometimes called casein.

Caseous Resembling cheese.

Certified Milk Milk certified as pure by a Board of Health.

Colostrum   The fluid secreted by the mammary gland before birth *(colostrum gravidarum)* or for the first few days after birth *(colostrum puerperium).* In human females it is thick and yellowish and contains more protein, less sugar, and much less fat than the milk which is formed later, several days after childbirth.

Condensed milk   Partly evaporated and sweetened milk.

Curd   Milk coagulum. Milk coagulated in the stomach forming what is known as a "curd."

Diabetic milk   Milk with a small amount of lactose.

Doula   One or more individuals, often female, who give psychological encouragement and physical assistance to the newly-delivered mother. (Term first used in modern context—Raphael, 1966.)

Draught   (See *ejection reflex*)

Ejection reflex   A reflex which ejects the milk from the mammary gland. As the infant sucks, nerves in the nipple send "messages" to the brain which are transmitted to the pituitary gland and trigger the release of a hormone called *oxytocin* into the bloodstream. Within seconds, this chemical stimulates the contraction of a network of myoepithelial cells around the "pools" (alveoli) where the milk is stored. This causes the ejection of that milk from the distal parts of the duct system within the breast to the terminal dilated areas beneath the areola, where it becomes available to the suckling child. (See *draught, let-down*)

Embryo   An organism in the earlier stages of gestation. In the human being the organism is called an embryo up to the third month. Thereafter it is referred to as a *fetus.*

Engorgement   Distention of the breasts with milk, usually occurring in the beginning of lactation when the breasts sometimes become hard, lumpy and painful. This condition generally disappears after a few days of frequent milking by hand expression or by the infant's sucking.

Episiotomy   A medial or lateral incision of the vulva during childbirth, performed by the delivering physician ostensibly to avoid undue lacerations.

Establishment of lactation The point at which the human infant/mother feeding relationship is in balance, whereby the infant's needs for nutrition and sucking and the mother's milk supply and ejection reflex are complementary. This usually occurs between 2 and 6 weeks after birth.

Estrogen Any of a group of female hormones occurring naturally or supplied from synthetically prepared matter which is capable of producing estrus in the female.

Estrus, -rous Period of sexual excitement and receptivity; heat, when applied to female non-human mammals.

Ferment milk A diastatic, enzyme-like ferment found in milk.

Flash method Modern method of pasteurizing milk.

Foetus (or fetus) The later stages of development during gestation of an animal organism in the egg or womb. In human beings this period extends from the beginning of the third month of pregnancy until birth.

Follicle-stimulating hormone (FSH) A hormone produced in the anterior lobe of the pituitary gland which functions to regulate the growth of the Graafian follicle, possibly the level of prolactin and, in the male, to stimulate the production of spermatozoa.

Foremilk The milk obtained first from the gland, as opposed to the *hindmilk*, that part which is withdrawn by the infant last. The foremilk may contain as little as one percent fat; the hind milk as much as ten percent.

Furlough For Reproduction (F.F.R.) That period of time suggested as (minimum) six months or (better) one year when the mother is given leave from her job for childbirth, breastfeeding, and infant care. After this leave of absence, with or without pay, she can return to her position either full or part-time.

Galact-, galacto- Pertaining to milk or milky fluids.

Galactacrasia An abnormal composition of milk.

Galactagogin The hormone of the placenta acting as a galactagogue.

Galactagogue An agent which promotes the flow of milk.

Galactase An enzyme in milk which activates the hydrolysis or breakdown of casein in the stomach during digestion.

Galactemia, galacthemia Milky condition of the blood.

Galactic Pertaining to a galaxy or the Milky Way, also the stimulation and secretion of milk.

Galactidrosis A milklike sweat.

Galactin A synonym for a lactogenic hormone; a basic amorphous substance in milk; prolactin.

Galactoblast A body found in the colostrum in mammary acini which contain fat globules.

Galactocele A cystic tumor in the ducts of the breast containing milk or milky fluids.

Galactogenous Suitable for or furthering the production of milk.

Galactogogue An agent promoting secretion of milk.

Galactoma Cystic tumor of the female breast; galactocele.

Galactometer Device for measuring the amount of cream in milk by its specific gravity for the purpose of determining fat content; galactoscope; lactometer; lactoscope.

Galactophagous Feeding upon milk.

Galactophore A duct carrying milk.

Galactophorous Conveying milk (galactophorous duct).

Galactophthisis Debility and emaciation as a result of excessive milk secretion.

Galactophygous Arresting the flow of milk as by hormonal injection following birth.

Galactopoiesis The production and secretion of milk in the mammary gland.

Galactopoietic (-poetic) The ability of a hormone or any substance to enhance an already established milk secretion; having a part in the secretion of milk.

Galactopyra A febrile condition often affecting dairy cows immediately after calving, causing somnolence and paralysis; also known as milk fever.

Galactorrhea (-rhoea) Continuation of lactation, or flow of milk at intervals after cessation of nursing; excessive flow of milk; spontaneous production of milk without a preceding pregnancy.

Galactoschesia (-schesis) A stopping of the milk secretion.

Galactose A simple sugar obtained in one form from milk sugar and in another from mucilages.

Galactosemia A congenital metabolic disorder in the infant, in which there is an increased galactose level in the blood, causing the failure of the infant to thrive.

Galactosis A secretion of milk.

Galactostasis Cessation or checking of milk secretion.

Galactotherapy Treatment of a nursing infant by drugs administered to the mother; galactopathy.

Galactotoxin A poison produced in milk by bacteria.

Galactotoxism Milk poisoning.

Galactotrophy Feeding with nothing but milk.

Galaxy The Milky Way, millions of stars which merge into a luminous band across the sky.

Gastroenteritis Inflammation of the stomach and intestines.

Geophagy   The practice of eating earth or clay, often occurring during pregnancy.

Hexenmilch   (See *neonatal secretion*)

Homogenized milk   Milk in which the fats are combined with the body of the milk.

Hypergalactia   Excess lactation.

Hypogalactia   Inadequate lactation.

Kumiss (Kumyss, Koumiss)   Cow's milk after fermentation with sugar and yeast; fermented mare's or camel's milk.

Lac   Milk, milky medicinal substance.

Lactagogue   An agent which induces secretion of milk.

Lactation   The formation and secretion of milk. The period of milk production.

Lacteal   Relating, producing, resembling milky fluid.

Lacteal gland   Lymph gland situated upon a lacteal vessel.

Lactenin   Nitrogenous substance present in milk that inhibits bacterial growth.

Lacteous   Milky, white.

Lactescence, Lactescent   Milkiness, milky appearance.

Lactic   Of or relating to milk.

Lactic acid   An acid formed when milk sours. Obtained from sour milk or whey.

Lactic casein   An acid casein precipitated from milk by lactic acid.

Lactic fermentation   Fermentation which produces lactic acid.

Lactiferous   Secreting or conveying milk.

Lactiferous gland   The mammary gland.

Lactific   Relating to milk.

Lactifuge   Stopping milk secretion. Syn: ischoglactic.

Lactify   To transform by lactic fermentation.

Lactigenous   Producing milk.

Lactigerous   See *lactiferous.*

Lactin   Lactose, sugar of milk.

Lactinated   Containing or prepared with milk sugar.

Lactivorous   Feeding on milk. Living on milk.

Lactocele   Cystic breast tumor due to occlusion of a milk duct.

Lactobacillus bifidus   The most numerous organism in the intestinal flora of the newborn infant.

Lactocrit   Device to measure fatty substances in milk.

Lactodensimeter   Device to measure the specific gravity of milk.

Lactogen   Any agent, particularly a hormone, that stimulates the secretion of milk.

Lactogenesis   The initiation of lactation.

Lactogenic hormones   Pituitary gland hormones which activate and stimulate secretion in the mammary glands. (See *prolactin*)

Lactiglobulin   A protein found in milk.

Lactolase   An enzyme forming lactic acid.

Lactolin   Condensed or evaporated milk.

Lactorrhea   Discharge of milk between nursings and after weaning of offspring.

Lactoscope   Device for determining the quality of milk.

Lactose   The principal sugar in milk.

Lactovegetarian   Of or relating to a diet of milk and vegetables and sometimes eggs.

Let-down reflex   (See *ejection reflex*)

Luteotrophin   A hormone that regulates production of progesterone and stimulates lactation; prolactin.

Mammae   The female breasts; milk-secreting glands in the female mammal.

Mammal   That class of animals including man that feeds its young with milk from the female mammary glands, that has a body more or less covered with hair, and that with the exception of the monotremes brings forth living young rather than eggs.

Mammary   Pertaining to the breast.

Mammary glands   Milk-producing glands in the breasts of all mammals. In females, these glands are enlarged and develop lobules, or milk-secreting sacs which contain a network of ducts that empty the milk into the nipple. In males they are rudimentary and underdeveloped.

Mastitis   Inflammation and abscess in the breast. There are many varieties. Two of the principal ones are *superficial mastitis,* an infection of the skin or the areola which spreads into the breast, and *intramammary mastitis,* a localized retention of milk within the engorged breast, which becomes infected and results in cellulitis and the formation of an abscess.

Matrescence   The state of becoming-a-mother, or motherhood as a new experience for the individual. This change of roles is both a biological and a cultural phenomenon. The transition period varies in length of time from culture to culture.

Matzoon (Armenian)   Milk with a ferment containing lactic acid, bacilli, and other organisms resembling yogurt.

Milk bank   Lactarium, where breast milk is collected and stored.

Milk casein   Milk prepared with a large quantity of casein and fat, but little sugar and salts.

Milk fever   A synonym for puerperal fever. The fever associated with inflammation or engorgement of the breasts.

Milk leg   A folk term for acute edema of the leg following childbirth; also phlebitis occasionally following parturition, characterized by swelling and whiteness of the leg.

Milk-line   A small band of cells, seen in the human embryo as early as three weeks, which becomes raised and extends down both sides of the body in both sexes from the armpit to the inner thigh. When embryological development goes awry, the individual may be born with one or more supernumerary nipples anywhere along this line.

Milk poisoning   Poisoning in man from the ingestion of impure milk. Usual symptoms include headache, vertigo, thirst, vomiting, indigestion, diarrhea, skin eruptions and possible collapse.

Milk sickness (or "trembles")   A disease of cattle and sheep transmitted to man through milk and butter, characterized by pain, vomiting, constipation and muscular tremors. Formerly common in some parts of the Middle West where cattle had been poisoned by eating certain kinds of snakeroot.

Milksop   An unmanly, effeminate man or youth.

Milk teeth   First or deciduous teeth.

Milk tumor   Tumor formed by retention of milk in the mammary gland.

Modified milk   Water and lactose mixed with cream.

Montgomery's glands   Twenty to twenty-four glands in the areola that secrete fluids which lubricate the nipple area.

Mother's milk   Milk from the mammary gland of a woman.

Natural children   Children which the natural mother (as opposed to the adoptive mother) has borne, biological children.

Neonatal secretion   (Also called *hexenmilch, lait de sorcière,* witch's milk.) A colostral secretion which occurs in some newborn infants three or more days after birth and continues until the twentieth day. It is thought to be a reaction to maternal hormones which pass the placental barrier and load the infant's system shortly before birth.

Nipple The conical projection in the center of the mamma containing the outlets of the milk ducts. Also called "papilla."

Non-gendered female Term used by Ray Birdwhistell and others to designate the non-reproducing female. This female may or may not be married. She may or may not be capable of producing young, but does not do so. Terms used for these women vary from the derogatory "old maid" to the more positive "auntie" (honorific).

Non-nutritional sucking The act of sucking a breast which has little or no secretion, usually done to calm or quiet an infant.

Non-puerperal lactation The production of milk in the absence of childbirth.

Non-puerperal induced lactation Lactation which is induced mechanically or by an infant's sucking in the absence of pregnancy or childbirth.

Non-puerperal women A term referring to females who have not experienced childbirth.

Nullipara A female who has never given birth as opposed to a primipara or multipara.

Oxytocin The pituitary hormone released from the posterior part of the gland into the bloodstream as a response to an infant's sucking. It flows to the mammary gland where it acts on the myoepithelial cells surrounding the alveoli, causing them to contract and release the milk so that it becomes available to the suckling child. (See *ejection reflex*)

Pasteurized milk Milk heated for thirty minutes at 143–158° F. (60 to 70 C.) to kill living bacteria.

Patrescence The state of becoming-a-father, a co-term to the word "matrescence." It is used to define the male role change when he first experiences paternity. Both terms are used primarily in the cultural sense similar to the general usage of "adolescence." Fatherhood occurs at different time designations and need not coincide with the actual birth of a man's child

Peptonized milk Milk partly digested with pepsin and hydrochloric acid, or pancreatic extract and sodium bicarbonate.

Pituitary gland A small, oval endocrine gland attached to the base of the brain, which secretes many hormones, several of which are critical for breastfeeding. The anterior lobe of the pituitary gland secretes prolactin, the hormone associated with lactation. The posterior lobe secretes oxytocin, the hormone critical in the ejection of milk.

Placental lactogen Hormones produced by the placenta which affect lactation.

Progesterone A hormone of the ovary which in addition to other functions prepares the uterus for the fertilized egg and maintains pregnancy.

Prolactin A pivotal hormone in lactation. (See *luteotrophin*)

Protein milk Milk with high protein and low carbohydrate and fat content.

Protractility of the nipple The extension, protrusion, and lengthening of the nipple induced by the sucking action of the infant, which normally is sufficiently long enough to allow the nipple to extend well back into the baby's mouth. If protractility is insufficient, the infant will not be stimulated to suck, and breastfeeding is affected.

Rebound secretion The term used to describe the small amount of secretion found in the breast after weaning, or, if lactation is suppressed, after childbirth.

Reestablishment of lactation (Also called relactation) The process of restimulating the milk supply of a female who has interrupted the cycle of pregnancy, childbirth, and lactation for any length of time. The sucking of the infant, the ingestion of liquids etc. may combine to bring back the milk supply.

Rites de passage Rituals, rites, and cultural practices surrounding the arrival of key periods in the life cycle, such as birth, puberty, marriage, and death. These rites develop an emotional state which facilitates bridging the gap between the "old" and the "new." (See *matrescence* and *patrescence*)

Ropy milk   Milk which has become viscid.

Skimmed milk   Milk after the removal of the cream.

Sour milk   Milk with lactic acid, caused by lactic acid bacteria.

Sphincter of the nipple   Contractile tissue around the nipple which keeps the milk in until it is released by the sucking of the infant.

Sterilized milk   Milk boiled to kill bacteria.

Successful lactation   In a non-Western, developing country where bottles and artificial milk are not predictable, successful lactation occurs when the baby obtains sufficient milk and thrives. The author has defined success in Western cultures where proper refrigeration, pasturization, etc. are predictable, as that period of time deemed as adequate and sufficient by the mother. It can but need not include supplementary feeding. It is a voluntary act by the mother terminated at her discretion. Michael Newton (1961) writes that "a woman may be said to lactate successfully if she continues to feed her baby entirely by the breast without difficulty and the baby remains healthy and gains weight."

Sucking   The action of the lips and tongue which produces a partial vacuum in the mouth. In the infant it is the action which draws the milk from the breast and at the same time stimulates the production of milk.

Suckling   An infant that is feeding from the breast. The act of sucking at the breast.

Sugar of milk   Lactose.

Tubercles of Montgomery   (See *Montgomery's glands*)

Tyrosis   Cheesy degeneration from the curdling of milk; vomiting of cheesy substance by infants.

Unsuccessful lactation Breastfeeding (in Western affluent cultures with a predictable use of artificial methods), which is terminated against the will of the mother or when her milk supply fails before she planned to stop. Since lactation failure does not lead to the death of the infant in these areas, it can be defined in terms of the emotional as well as the physical needs of the mother and the infant.

Uterine milk White milklike substance between the gravid uterus and the villi of the placenta. An early theory of the origin of milk stated that milk was uterine in origin and was carried by special vessels to the mammary gland and so the uterine milk which fed the fetus was also available to the suckling baby. (Also called the "chyle" theory.)

Uviol milk Milk sterilized by ultraviolet rays.

Vegetable milk The latex of plants.

Whey The liquid left after milk has been coagulated, as in the making of cheese.

Witch's milk (See *neonatal secretion*)

Yogurt Curdled milk containing lactic acid. It is formed by boiling the milk, cooling it, and adding a culture (yogurt) of acid-forming bacteria.

BIBLIOGRAPHY

Alexander, Shana
1962   "Belle's Baby—225 Pounds and All Elephant." *Life*
(May 11) 104–120.

Allee, W. C.
1958   *The Social Life of Animals.* (Rev. ed. of 1938 publication.) Boston: Beacon Press.

Altmann, Margaret
1961   "Sex Dynamics Within Kinships of Free-ranging Wild
Ungulates." Paper read at the American Association
for the Advancement of Science Symposium on Incest,
Denver, December 30.
1963   "Naturalistic Studies of Maternal Care in Moose and
Elk." *Maternal Behavior in Mammals,* Harriet L.
Rheingold, ed. New York: John Wiley & Sons, Inc.

Bain, Katherine
1948   "The Incidence of Breast Feeding in Hospitals in the
United States." *Pediatrics* 2:313–320.

Barry, J. M.
1957   "The Synthesis of Milk." *Scientific American* 197, no.
4:121–128.

Bateson, Catherine
1972   Personal communications.

Bateson, Gregory, and Margaret Mead
1951   "First Days in the Life of a New Guinea Baby." *New
York University Film Library,* 16mm sound, 19 minutes.

Blauvelt, Helen
1955   "Dynamics of the Mother-Newborn Relationship in
Goats." *Group Process, Transactions of the First Conference,* 1954, Bertram Schaffner, ed. New York: The
Josiah Macy, Jr. Foundation.
1956   "Neonate-mother Relationship in Goat and Man."

*Group Processes, Transactions of the Second Confer-
ence*, 1955, Bertram Schaffner, ed. New York: Josiah
Macy, Jr. Foundation.
1962   "Capacity of a Human Neonate Reflex to Signal Future
Response by Present Action." *Child Development*
33:21–28.

Bowlby, John
1952   "Maternal Care and Mental Health." *World Health Organization Monograph Series No. 2*, Geneva: Palais des
Nations.

Brody, Sylvia
1956   *Patterns of Mothering: Maternal Influence During Infancy*. New York: International Universities Press, Inc.

Budin, P. C.
1907   *The Nursling*. London: Caxton. (Ref. from Evans &
MacKeith p. 60 in Kon and Cowie, *Milk: the Mammary
Gland and Its Secretion.*)

Carrington, Richard T. M.
1959   *Elephants*. New York: Basic Books.

Davies, J. N. P.
1949   "Sex Hormone Upset in Africans." *British Medical
Journal* ii:676–679.

Davis, Herbert V., Robert R. Sears, Herbert C. Miller, and Ar-
thur J. Brodbeck
1948   "Effect of Cup, Bottle and Breast Feeding on Oral Activities of Newborn Infants." *Pediatrics* 2:549–558.

Deanesly, R. and A. S. Parkes
1951   "Colloque internationale—centennial nationale de re-
cherche scientifique 32:174.

Deem, H. M., and M. McGeorge
1958   "Breast Feeding." *New Zealand Medical Journal*
57:539–556.

De Gonzalez, Nacie L. Solien
1964 "Lactation and Pregnancy: A Hypothesis." *American Anthropologist* 66:873–878.

Deutsch, H.
1945 *The Psychology of Women.* New York: Grune & Stratton.

Douglas, J. W. B.
1950 "The Extent of Breast Feeding in Great Britain in 1946, with Special Reference to the Health and Survival of Children." *Journal of Obstetrics and Gynaecology of the British Empire* 57:335–361.

Douglas-Hamilton, Iain
1972 Personal communications.

Eisenbud, Jule
1964 "A recently found carving as a breast symbol." *American Anthropologist* 66, 1:141–147.

Ely, F. and W. E. Petersen
1941 "Factors Involved in the Ejection of Milk." *Journal of Dairy Science* 24:211–223.

Etkin, William, editor
1964 *Social Behavior and Organization Among Vertebrates.* Chicago: University of Chicago Press.

Fass, Elias N.
1962 "Is Bottle Feeding of Milk a Factor in Dental Caries?" *Journal of Dentistry for Children* 29:245–251.

Finch, Clement A.
1969 "Iron Metabolism." *Nutrition Today,* Summer.
1967 "Iron Metabolism." *The Lancet,* June 17.

Firth, Raymond
1936 *We the Tikopia: A Sociological Study of Kinship in Primitive Polynesia.* London: George Allen and Unwin Ltd.
1956 "Ceremonies for Children and Social Frequency In Tikopia." *Oceania,* 27, 1.

Ford, Clellan S., and Frank A. Beach
  1951 *Patterns of Sexual Behavior*. New York: Harper and
        Brothers Publishers.

Foss, F. G. L. and D. Short
  1951 "Journal of Obstetrics and Gynaecology of the British
        Empire" 58:35 (Cited by Newton in Kon and Cowie.)

Frank, Lawrence
  1945 "Feeding of the Newborn." Report of the conference
        of the committee on infancy and childhood. *Psychoso-
        matic Medicine* 7:169–172.

Franklin, John
  1923 "Narrative of a Journey to the Shores of the Polar Sea.
        (Quoted in Ploss and Barteles, M. 1935 *Women*, 3:216,
        London.)

Gates, Helen
  1972 "Abnormal Lactation." (In press.)

Gesell, Arnold, and Frances L. Ilg
  1937 *Feeding Behavior of Infants: a Pediatric Approach to
        the Mental Hygiene of Early Life*. Philadelphia: J. B.
        Lippincott Company.

Gideon, Helen
  1960 "A Baby Is Born in the Punjab." *American Anthropolo-
        gist* 64:1220–1234.

Gordon, Richard E., Katherine K. Gordon, and Max Gunther
  1960 *The Split-Level Trap*. New York: Random House.

Greenway, P. J.
  1937 "Artificially Induced Lactation in Humans." *East Afri-
        can Medical Journal* 13:346.

Gunther, M.
  1955 "Instinct and the Nursing Couple." *The Lancet*
        268:575–578.
  1970 *Infant Feeding*. London: Methuen & Co. Ltd.

György, P.
  1961 "Orientation in Infant Feeding." *Federation Proceedings* 20:169–176.
  1971 "Biochemical Aspects." *The American Journal of Clinical Nutrition* 24: August, 970–975.

Halban, J.
  1905 "Die innere Secretion von Ovarium und Placenta und ihre Bedeutung für die Function der Milchdrüse." *Archiv für Gynäkologie* 75:353–441.

Harlow, Harry F., Margaret K. Harlow, and Ernst W. Hansen
  1963 "The Maternal Affectional System of Rhesus Monkeys." *Maternal Behavior in Mammals*, H. L. Rheingold, ed. New York: John Wiley & Sons, Inc.

Heinstein, Martin I.
  1963 "Influence of Breast Feeding on Children's Behavior." *Children* 10, 3:93–97.

Holt, L. Emmett, Jr.
  1927 *The Care and Feeding of Children*. New York: Appleton. (Rev. eds. 1929, 1937, 1943.)

Holt, L. Emmett, Sr.
  1894 *The Care and Feeding of Children*. New York: Appleton. (Rev. eds. 1903, 1909, 1910, 1918.)

Huang, Shi-Shung & Theodore M. Bayless
  1968 "Milk and Lactose Intolerance in Healthy Orientals." *Science* 160:83 April.

Hytten, F. E., and A. M. Thomson
  1961 "Nutrition of the Lactating Woman." *Milk, the Mammary Gland and Its Secretion*, S. K. Kon and A. T. Cowie, eds. Vol. II. New York: Academic Press.

Jackson, E. B., Richard W. Olmsted, Alan Foord, Herbert Thoms, and Kate Hyden
  1948 "A Hospital Rooming-in Unit for Four Newborn Infants and Their Mothers: descriptive account of background, development, and procedures with a few preliminary observations." *Pediatrics* 1:28–43.

Jackson, Edith B., Louise C. Wilkin, and Harry Auerbach
  1956 "Statistical Report on Incidence and Duration of Breast-feeding in Relation to Personal, Social and Hospital Maternity Factors." *Pediatrics* 17:700–715.

Jay, Phyllis
  1963a "Mother-infant Relations in Langurs." *Maternal Behavior in Mammals*, Harriet L. Rheingold, ed. New York: John Wiley & Sons, Inc.
  1963b "The Indian Langur Monkey *(Presbytis entellus)*." *Primate Social Behavior*, Charles H. Southwick, ed. New York: Van Nostrand.

Jelliffe, Derrick B.
  1955 "Infant Nutrition in the Tropics and Subtropics." *World Health Organization, Geneva, Monograph Series No. 29.*
  1962 "Culture, Social Change and Infant Feeding, Current Trends in Tropical Regions." *American Journal of Clinical Nutrition* 10:19–45.

Josephs, Hugh
  1958 "Iron Absorption in Human Physiology." *Blood* 13:1–54.

Kon, S. K. and A. T. Cowie, eds.
  1961 *Milk: The Mammary Gland and Its Secretion.* New York: Academic Press.

La Leche League
  1963 *The Womanly Art of Breastfeeding.* Franklin Park, Illinois, La Leche League International.

LaMaze, F., and P. Vellay
  1952 "L'accouchement sans douleur par la méthode psychoprophylactique. Premiers résultats portant sur 500 cas." *Gazette médicale de France.* Paris, 29:1445–1460.

LaRoe, Else K.
  1947 *Care of the Breast.* New York: Froben Press Publishers.

Levy, David
  1937 "Thumb or Finger Sucking from the Psychiatric
        Angle." *Child Development* 8:99–101.

Lorenz, E.
  1929 "Über das Brustdrüsensekret des Neugeborenen. *Jahr-
        buch für Kinderheilkunde* 124:268–274.

Lorenz, Konrad
  1952 *King Solomon's Ring.* New York: Thomas Y. Crowell
        Company.

Lowenfeld, Margaret Frances, Sibyl Taite Widdows and Hazel
        H. Chodak Gregory
  1934 "Percentage of Fat in Human Milk." *The Lancet*
        1:1003–1006.

McCullough, G. L.
  1962 Paper delivered at a symposium on nutrition, Depart-
        ment of Human Ecology of Cambridge University, July
        7th and 8th.

McGeorge, Murray
  1960 "Current Trends In Breast Feeding." *The New Zea-
        land Medical Journal* 59:30–41.

Macy, I. G.
  1949 "Composition of Human Colostrum and Milk." *Ameri-
        can Journal of Diseases of Children* 78:589–603.

Malefijt, Annemarie de Waal
  1966 Personal communications.

Maslow, A. H., and I. Szilagyi-Kessler
  1946 "Security and Breast Feeding." *Journal of Abnormal
        and Social Psychology* 41:83–85.

Mayer, Gaston and Marc Klein
  1961 "Histology and Cytology of the Mammary Gland."
        Milk: The Mammary Gland and its Secretion. S. K. Kon
        and A. T. Cowie, eds. New York and London: Aca-
        demic Press.

Mead, Margaret
  1935 *Sex and Temperament.* New York: William Morrow.
  1954 "Some Theoretical Considerations on the Problem of Mother-child Separation." *American Journal of Orthopsychiatry* 24, 3:471–483.
  1966 Personal communications.

Mead, Margaret, and Niles R. Newton
  1967 "Cultural Patterning of Perinatal Behavior," Stephen A. Richardson & Alan Guttmacher, eds. *Childbearing —Its Social and Psychological Aspects.* Williams & Wilkins Co.

Meyer, Herman F.
  1958 "Infant-feeding Practices in Hospital Maternity Nurseries: a survey of 1,904 hospitals involving 2,225,000 newborn infants." *Pediatrics* 21, 2:288–297.

Middlemore, M. P.
  1941 *The Nursing Couple.* London: Hamish Hamilton.

Naish, F. Charlotte
  1956 *Breast Feeding, a Guide to the Natural Feeding of Infants.* London: Lloyd-Luke Ltd.

Netter, Frank
  1954 *The Ciba Collection of Medical Illustrations: A compilation of paintings on the normal and pathologic anatomy of the reproductive system.* Ernst Oppenheimer, ed. Vol. 2. Summit, New Jersey, Ciba Pharmaceutical Products, Inc.

Newton, Michael
  1961 "Human Lactation." *Milk, the Mammary Gland and Its Secretion,* S. K. Kon and A. T. Cowie, eds. New York: Academic Press.

Newton, Michael and Niles Rumely Newton
  1948 "The Let-down Reflex in Human Lactation." *The Journal of Pediatrics* 33:698–704.
  1962 "The Normal Course and Management of Lactation" *Clinical Obstetrics and Gynecology,* 5:1 March 44–63.

Newton, Niles
1952 "Nipple Pain and Nipple Damage." *The Journal of Pediatrics* 41, no. 4:411–423.
1955 *Maternal Emotions.* New York: Paul B. Hoeber, Inc.
1958 "The Influence of the Let-down Reflex in Breast Feeding on the Mother-child Relationship." *Marriage and Family Living* 20, no. 1:18–20.

Newton, Niles R., and M. Newton
1950a "Relationship of Ability to Breast Feed and Maternal Attitudes Toward Breast Feeding." *Pediatrics* 5:869–875.
1950b Relation of the Let-down Reflex to the Ability to Breast Feed." *Pediatrics* 5:726.
1951 "Recent Trends in Breast Feeding: a review." *American Journal of the Medical Sciences* 221:691–698.
1951 "Postpartum Engorgement of the Breast." *American Journal of Obstetrics and Gynecology* 61, 3:664–667.

Perez, A., P. Vela, R. Potter, and G. S. Masnick
1971 "Timing and Sequence of Resuming Ovulation and Menstruation After Childbirth." *Population Studies,* Vol. XXV:3:491 Nov.

Perlman, H. H. and A. M. Dannenberg
1942 "Excretion of Nicotine in Breast Milk and Urine from Cigarette Smoking." *Journal of the American Medical Association* 120:103.

Picard, Peter J.
1959 "Bottle Feeding as Preventive Orthodontics." *Journal of the California Dental Association and Nevada Dental Society* 35:90–95.

Rahill, M. A.
1957 "Mammary Gland Changes During Chlorpromazine therapy." *British Medical Journal* ii:806.

Raphael, Dana
1969 "Uncle Rhesus, Auntie Pachyderm, and Mom: All Sorts

and Kinds of Mothering." *Perspectives in Biology and Medicine,* Winter 290–297.

1966   "The Lactation-Suckling Process within a Matrix of Supportive Behavior." Unpublished Ph.D. dissertation, *Columbia University Micro-film* 69–15, 580.

1972   Reply to CA treatment. Papers on human reproduction. *Current Anthropology* 13:2 April 253.

Raynaud, Albert
1961   "Morphogenesis of the Mammary Gland." *Milk: the Mammary Gland and Its Secretion.* S. K. Kon and A. T. Cowie, eds. New York and London: Academic Press.

Read, Grantly Dick
1944   *Childbirth Without Fear.* New York: Harper & Brothers Publishers.

Ribble, Margaret A.
1943   *The Rights of Infants: Early Psychological Needs and their Satisfaction.* New York: Columbia University Press.

Richardson, Frank Howard
1953   *The Nursing Mother: A Guide to Successful Breast Feeding.* New York: Prentice-Hall, Inc.

Rosenblum, Leonard
1971   "Aunt-Infant Relations in Squirrel Monkeys." Paper presented at the annual American Anthropological Association Meeting. November 19.

Salk, Lee
1962   "Mother's Heartbeat as an Imprinting Stimulus." *Transactions of the New York Academy of Sciences, Series 2,* 24:753–764.

Schultze, O.
1892   Erste Anlage des Milchdrüsenapparates. *Anatomischer Anzeiger* 7:265–270.

Scientific American
1967   "50 and 100 years Ago," p. 10, March.

Skinner, Elliot
   1966   Personal communications.

Slijper, E. J.
   1962   *Whales.* New York: Basic Books.

Smith, Vearl R.
   1959   *The Physiology of Lactation,* 5th ed. Ames, Iowa: Iowa State University Press.

Soddy, K.
   1956   *Mental Health and Infant Development.* New York: Basic Books.

Spitz, Rene A.
   1945   "Hospitalism: an inquiry into the genesis of psychiatric conditions in early childhood." *Psychoanalytic Study of the Child* 1:53–74.

Spitz, Rene A., and K. M. Wolf
   1946a   "The Smiling Response: a contribution to the ontogenesis of social relations." *Genetic Psychology Monographs* 34:57–125.
   1946b   "Anaclitic Depression: an inquiry into the genesis of psychiatric conditions in early childhood II." *The Psychoanalytic Study of the Child* 2:313–342. New York: International Universities Press.

Spock, Benjamin
   1945   *The Common Sense Book of Baby and Child Care.* (Rev. ed. 1957.) New York: Duell, Sloan and Pearce, Inc.

Stevenson, S. S.
   1947   "Adequacy of Artificial Feeding in Infancy." *The Journal of Pediatrics* 31:616–630.

Sulman, F. G. & Winnik, H. Z.
   1966   "Hormonal Effects of Chlorpromazine." *The Lancet,* 1, 161.

Swidler, Warren & Nina Swidler
   1966   Personal communications.

Tyson, R. M., E. A. Schrader, & H. H. Perlman
 1937 "Drugs Transmitted Through Breast Milk. Part I: Laxatives." *The Journal of Pediatrics* 11, 824.

United States Children's Bureau of the Department of Health, Education and Welfare
 1914 *Infant Care*. Washington, D.C., U.S. Government Printing Office. (Rev. eds. 1921, 1932, 1938, 1940, 1942, 1945, 1951, 1955, 1957, 1963, 1964.)

Van Lawick-Goodall, Jane
 1968 "The Behaviour of Free-living Chimpanzees in the Gombe Stream Reserve." *Animal Behavior Monographs* Vol. 1; 3.

Van Gennep, Arnold
 1960 *The Rites of Passage*. Tr. by Monika B. Vizedom and Gabrielle L. Caffee. London: Routledge and Kegan Paul. (French edition 1909.)

Vellay, Pierre
 1959 *Childbirth Without Pain*. London: George Allen and Unwin Ltd.

Weischhoff, H. A.
 1940 "Artificial Stimulation of Lactation in Primitive Cultures." *Bulletin of the History of Medicine* 8:1403.

Winnik, H. Z. and L. Tennenbaum
 1955 "Apparition de galactorrhée au cours du traitement de largactil." *La Presse Médicale* 63:1092.

Wolfish, M. G.
 1953 "Acute Gastroenteritis: review of 518 cases treated at Hospital for Sick Children during 1951 and 1952." *The Journal of Pediatrics* 43:675–686.

World Health Organization Expert Committee on the Prevention of Cancer
 1964 "Prevention of Cancer." *World Health Organization Technical Report Series* no. 276:1–53. Geneva, World Health Organization.

INDEX

Adopt and breastfeed, 89–96, 105–15
American Indian rites, 27, 133
American patterns of childbirth and
    lactation, 16, 21–23, 25, 27–32,
    33, 45–46, 47–57
Animal associations, 44
Anthropological data, 131–38
Areola, 63–64
Artificial feeding, *see* Bottle feeding
ASPO, 165
Attachment, critical nature of, 75–78
    in animals, 76, 113
    between mother and infant, 76–78
Attitudes toward breastfeeding
    in America, 41–46
    of children, 46
    of females, 43–44, 75
    of males, 42–43
    of medical personnel, 29–30, 36–38
    and permissiveness, 51
    study of, 41–46
    to success, 38
Attraction of the newborn, 122–27

Baby, *see* Infant
Birth control during lactation, 83, 105
Borrowing babies, 94, 134
Bottle feeding
    benefits of, 56–57, 78, 80, 86
    change to, 47–57
    compared to breastfeeding, 75–87
    dangers of, 48–50
    and love, 34, 57, 78
    as "modern," "sterile," 48
    and personality of baby, 75
    protecting the mother, 17, 57, 77–
        78
    schedules for, 52–55
    and teeth, 81
    and thumb sucking, 82
Bowel movements in infants, 73, 79,
    109

Breast
    birth through menopause, 63–65
    development of, 61–67
    embryonic development, 61–62
    evolution of the, 59–61
    fat in the, 63, 66–67
    fluids of the, 72–74, 78–79
    function of the gland, 66–67
    as a machine, 45
    in males, 65–66
    during pregnancy, 64–65
Breastfeeding the adopted infant, 89–
    96, 105–15
    complication at, 106
    drugs during, 106
    effect of sucking during, 95–96
    preparation for, 93–94
    success at, 92, 107–09, 113–14
    supplements to, 106–09
    support during, 105, 109–11
    weaning after, 111–12
Breastfeeding
    advantage to infant, 79–85, 112–13
    advantage to mother, 83–86
    compared to bottle feeding, 75–87
    convenience of, 85–86
    duration of, 38–39
    ejection reflex in, 68–69
    failure at, 16, 33–34, 38
    "natural" mystique of, 37
    nutritional strain of, 84
    percentage incapable of, 67, 132
    in primitive cultures, 131–39
    protection for the mother, 86–87
    rituals of, 19, 20, 39–40, 132–33
    sharing with other women, 49
    success at, 34–36, 38–39, 141–42
    symbolic use of, 132–34
    taboos during, 132–34, 135–36
    weight gain in baby, 80
    weight gain in mother, 83–84
Bushman of South Africa, 134